T H E   B O O K   O F

BREAKFASTS & BRUNCHES

T H E   B O O K   O F

BREAKFASTS & BRUNCHES

KERENZA HARRIES

Photographed by
ALAN NEWNHAM

Book Express
Quality and Value in Every Book...

Specially produced for Book Express, Inc.,
Airport Business Center, 29 Kripes Road, East Granby, Connecticut, USA

This book was created by Merehurst Limited
Ferry House, 51/57 Lacy Road, Putney, London SW15 1PR

© 1990 Salamander Books Ltd.

ISBN: 0 86101 489 8

Commissioned and directed by Merehurst Limited
Managing Editor: Felicity Jackson
Designer: Sue Storey
Home Economist: Kerenza Harries
Photographer: Alan Newnham
Typeset by Angel Graphics
Colour separation by Magnum Graphics
Printed in Belgium by Proost International Book Production

CONTENTS

INTRODUCTION

The *Book of Breakfasts & Brunches* is full of unusual and exciting ideas for both of these meals. Starting with a selection of hearty breakfasts suitable for the most ravenous family, it continues with all kinds of novel ideas for special occasion breakfasts.

Nutritionists stress that breakfast is the most important meal of the day, so this book includes healthy recipes designed to fortify you for the remainder of the day.

Breakfast is a much neglected meal. All too often during the week, it consists of a quick bowl of cornflakes and a hasty cup of coffee. So when all the family are at home on the weekend, you have guests, or you are celebrating a special occasion, why not, with the help of this book turn breakfast into a social time.

The civilized meal of brunch, combining both breakfast and lunch, so loved by the Americans, Australians and English, is reminiscent of the splended country house breakfasts served by the English aristocracy in the 1800s. Breakfast for their house guests ran from early in the morning until the final stragglers appeared later in the day, and there was a wide choice of sausages, bacon, fish and egg dishes set out on the sideboard. Brunch is a delightfully informal way of entertaining either a small or large group of people, especially when the age groups are mixed.

Brunches can include anything from the traditional breakfast fare of eggs and bacon to luncheon foods like salads, cheese and fruit desserts. For informal brunches the dishes are ones that can be prepared with a minimum of fuss—ideal when you have guests staying for the weekend, a family gathering or casual entertaining if friends pop in.

All the food for summer brunches is suitable for eating outdoors with either fingers or forks. The secret of successful brunch parties for large numbers is in choosing a whole range of simple dishes rather than one or two complicated ones that are going to need a lot of last minute attention once your guests have arrived. The recipes for summer brunches and party brunches can be mixed and matched to feed any number of people.

To finish there is a choice of brunch and breakfasts drinks, including champagne fizz, spiced tea and infusions.

With over 100 tempting recipes all beautifully illustrated in color, you will find that breakfast and brunch will never be the same again. Bon appétit!

Crusty Crumpets

6 crumpets or English muffins
1 (6-1/2-oz.) can pink salmon
1 tablespoon plus 1 teaspoon mayonnaise
3 green onions, finely sliced
1 cup crumbled Red Leicester cheese
** (4 oz.)**
Few drops hot-pepper sauce
Salt and pepper to taste
Sprigs of watercress to garnish

Toast crumpets or muffins on both sides. Preheat broiler. Drain salmon and remove skin and bones. In a medium-size bowl, flake salmon. Mix in mayonnaise, green onions, 3/4 cup of cheese and season with hot-pepper sauce and salt and pepper. Spoon salmon mixture on top of crumpets or muffins and sprinkle with remaining cheese. Broil until golden and bubbly. Serve immediately, garnished with sprigs of watercress.

Makes 6 servings.

Egg & Mushroom Benedict

2 English muffins
1/2 cup herb butter, see Note
4 large shiitake or mushrooms
4 eggs plus 1 extra egg yolk
2 tablespoons white wine vinegar
1 tablespoon water
8 tablespoons butter, melted
Salt and pepper to taste
Sprigs of chervil to garnish

Split muffins in half and toast on both sides. Preheat broiler. In a small saucepan, melt herb butter and generously brush both sides of each mushroom. Broil 2 minutes on each side. Bring a large pan of water to simmering point and carefully crack 4 eggs into water. Poach 3 to 4 minutes, then remove with a slotted spoon and drain on paper towels. In a small saucepan, bring vinegar and water to a boil and reduce by half. In a blender or food processor fitted with the metal blade, process egg yolk 30 seconds, pouring in hot vinegar reduction; slowly add melted butter. Season with salt and pepper. Place a mushroom on top of each muffin half, top with a poached egg and spoon sauce over egg. Garnish with sprigs of chervil and serve immediately.

Makes 4 servings.

Note: To prepare herb butter, mix 1 tablespoon of finely chopped fresh herbs and 1/2 cup of softened butter.

———— Sausage & Apple Braid ————

1/2 (17-1/4-oz.) package frozen puff
   pastry (1 sheet)
10 ounces pork sausage
1 egg, beaten
1 onion, very finely chopped
2 apples, very finely chopped
3/4 cup dried herb stuffing mix
Beaten egg to glaze
1 tablespoon sesame seeds
Apple slices and sage leaves to garnish

Preheat oven to 400F (205C). Roll out pastry to a 18" x 14" rectangle and let stand. In a large bowl, mix sausage, 1 beaten egg, onion, apples and stuffing mix. Spoon sausage filling down center of pastry, leaving about 2-1/2 inches of pastry at top and bottom and 4 inches on each side of filling. Brush edges of pastry with beaten egg and fold top and bottom over filling. Make 3-inch cuts at 1/2-inch intervals down each side of pastry. Fold 1 strip over filling from alternate sides until filling is completely enclosed. Brush completely with beaten egg and sprinkle with sesame seeds. Place on a baking sheet and bake in preheated oven 30 minutes, until golden. Serve hot or cold, garnished with apple slices and sage leaves.

Makes 6 to 8 servings.

Breakfast Kabobs

12 bacon slices
2 ounces Emmenthaler cheese
16 cherry tomatoes
16 button mushrooms
1 tablespoon vegetable oil
1 teaspoon tomato paste
1 teaspoon Worcestershire sauce
1 teaspoon prepared hot mustard
1 teaspoon soy sauce
Toast to serve

Preheat broiler. Cut bacon slices in half.
Cut cheese in 24 chunks and wrap a
piece of bacon around each. Thread
bacon rolls, mushrooms and tomatoes
alternately onto skewers, starting and
ending with a bacon roll. In a small
bowl, mix oil, tomato paste, Worcestershire sauce, mustard and soy sauce and
brush over kabobs. Broil 5 minutes,
turning frequently, and brushing with
any extra sauce. Serve immediately
with toast.

Makes 4 servings.

Oatmeal Chive Crepes

1/2 cup all-purpose flour
1/3 cup regular rolled oats, ground
Pinch salt
6 large eggs
1-1/4 cups milk
2 tablespoons chopped fresh chives
8 thin slices smoked ham
2 tablespoons butter
1 to 2 tablespoons half and half
Salt and pepper to taste

Sift flour, oats and salt into a large bowl. Add 2 eggs, milk and 1 tablespoon of chives and beat to form a smooth batter. Heat a griddle and brush with oil. Pour in enough batter to prepare a 6-inch crepe and cook 1 minute. Turn crepe over and top with a slice of ham. Keep warm between 2 plates set over a pan of simmering water. Repeat with remaining batter. Melt butter in a small saucepan. In a small bowl, beat remaining eggs and pour into butter. Cook over low heat, stirring constantly, until thickened. Remove from heat and stir in remaining chives and half and half. Season with salt and pepper. Spoon eggs into center of each crepe and roll up. Serve at once.

Makes 8 servings.

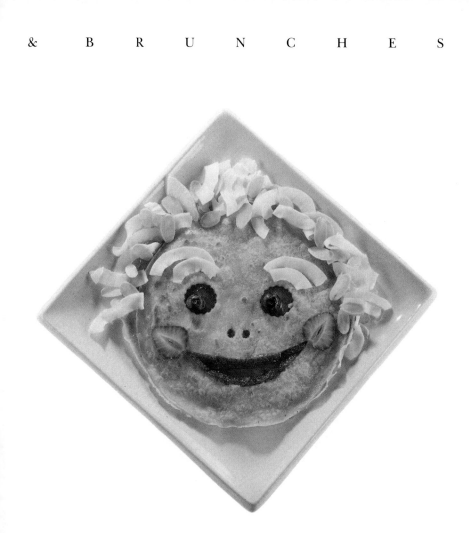

Pancake Faces

1 cup all-purpose flour
Pinch salt
1 egg
1-1/4 cups milk
Grated peel of 1/2 lemon
Vegetable oil
3 tablespoons strawberry conserve,
    sieved
2 teaspoons lemon juice
8 blueberries
1-3/4 cups shredded sweetened coconut
4 strawberries, sliced
1/2 cup toasted sliced almonds

Sift flour and salt into a large bowl. Add egg, milk and lemon peel and beat to form a smooth batter. Heat a griddle and brush with oil. Pour in some batter and cook 1 minute, until underside of pancake is golden. Turn over and cook other side 1 minute. Keep warm between 2 plates set over a pan of simmering water. Repeat with remaining batter. In a small bowl, mix conserve and lemon juice. Cut out eyes, 2 nostrils and a mouth from 4 pancakes. Spread remaining pancakes with conserve mixture and top with pancake faces. Place a blueberry in each eye, shredded coconut as eyebrows and slices of strawberries for cheeks and mouth. Mix remaining coconut and almonds and arrange around edge of pancake face as hair. Serve at once.

Makes 4 servings.

Rosti

1-1/2 pounds boiling potatoes, scrubbed
1 small onion
4 bacon slices
1/4 cup Austrian smoked cheese
Salt and pepper to taste
3 tablespoons butter

Place potatoes in a pan of salted water, bring to a boil and simmer 5 minutes. Drain and cool. Coarsely grate potatoes and onion into a large bowl. Cut bacon in very thin strips. Cut cheese in small chunks and, using 2 forks, toss bacon and cheese with potato mixture; season with salt and pepper. Melt butter in a large skillet and add grated mixture. Cook over medium heat 10 to 15 minutes, then press together well. Turn over and cook other side 5 minutes. Turn out onto a warmed plate, cut in wedges and serve at once.

Makes 4 servings.

Spanish Omelet

8 bacon slices
1 tablespoon olive oil
1 tablespoon butter
1 onion, chopped
1 potato, cooked, diced
8 button mushrooms, quartered
8 cherry tomatoes, quartered
1 tablespoon chopped fresh parsley
4 large eggs, beaten
1 tablespoon cold water
Salt and pepper to taste
1/2 cup shredded Cheddar cheese (2 oz.)
Sprigs of parsley to garnish

In a medium-size skillet, cook 6 bacon slices until crisp, then cut in strips. Set aside. In a large skillet, heat olive oil and butter. Add onion and cook over low heat 2 minutes. Chop remaining bacon slices and add to onion. Cook 2 minutes. Add potato and mushrooms and stir well, then add tomatoes and chopped parsley. In a small bowl, whisk eggs with cold water. Season with salt and pepper and pour into skillet. Cook over gentle heat 3 to 4 minutes, until bottom is golden and set. Sprinkle grated cheese over omelet; broil until mixture is golden and puffy. Cut in 4 portions and sprinkle with bacon strips and garnish with sprigs of parsley.

Makes 4 servings.

BLT

12 bacon slices
1/4 cup mayonnaise
1 teaspoon German mustard
1 teaspoon chopped fresh parsley
2 large tomatoes, thinly sliced
8 slices whole-wheat bread
Lettuce leaves

In a large skillet, cook bacon until crisp
and golden. Drain well on paper towels.
In a small bowl, mix mayonnaise, mustard and parsley and spread on bread.
Arrange tomato slices over 4 slices of
bread, then arrange 3 bacon slices and
some lettuce on top. Top with remaining slices of bread, mayonnaise side
down. Cut in half and serve at once.

Makes 4 servings.

Salami & Melon Snack

4 slices pumpernickel bread
2 tablespoons butter, softened
12 thin slices salami
1/2 small melon
1 tablespoon mayonnaise
1 tablespoon dairy sour cream
1 teaspoon capers, chopped
1/2 teaspoon pink peppercorns, crushed

Spread bread with butter and arrange 3 salami slices on each. Remove seeds and peel melon; slice thinly in 12 pieces. Arrange 3 slices on each sandwich. In a small bowl, mix mayonnaise and sour cream and spoon onto melon. Sprinkle with capers and peppercorns.

Makes 4 servings.

Ham & Egg Loaf

1 pound cooked ham
3 ounces small mushrooms (about 1 cup)
3/4 cup dried stuffing mix
5 eggs
2/3 cup half and half
2 teaspoons soy sauce
1 tablespoon chopped fresh parsley

Mince ham and mushrooms. In a large bowl, combine minced ham and mushrooms and stuffing mix. Place 3 eggs in a medium-size saucepan of cold water. Bring to a boil and simmer 10 minutes, until hard. Plunge into cold water and remove shells. Meanwhile, preheat oven to 375F (190C). In a small bowl, beat remaining eggs, half and half, soy sauce and parsley. Pour into ham mixture and stir well. Place 1/2 of mixture in a 9" x 5" loaf pan and arrange hard-cooked eggs down center. Top with remaining ham mixture and bake in preheated oven 60 minutes. Cool completely, turn out and thickly slice.

Makes 4 servings.

Note: Serve with crusty rolls.

Cheesy Bread

3 cups self-rising flour
1 teaspoon baking powder
1/4 teaspoon salt
1 teaspoon sugar
1 cup milk
2 teaspoons prepared mustard
1/2 cup shredded Cheddar cheese (2 oz.)
1/2 cup shredded Gloucester cheese with
   chives (2 oz.)
4 tablespoons butter, softened
2 tablespoons half and half
2 teaspoons dry sherry
2 teaspoons chpped fresh chives

Preheat oven to 425F (220C). Dust a baking sheet with flour. Sift flour, baking powder, salt and sugar into a large bowl. In a glass measure, combine milk and mustard and pour into dry ingredients. Mix quickley to form a soft dough. Place dough on prepared baking sheet. Press out to a circle about 1-1/2 inches thick. Using a sharp knife, mark in 8 wedges. Sprinkle with Cheddar cheese and bake in preheated oven 10 minutes. Lower oven temperature to 400F (205C) and bake 20 minutes more, until well risen and golden. Cool slightly. In a blender or a food processor fitted with the metal blade, process double Gloucester cheese, butter, half and half, sherry and chives until mixed. Spoon into a serving dish and serve with hot bread.

Makes 8 servings.

Corn Fritters

1/2 cup cornmeal
1/2 cup all-purpose flour
2 large eggs
2/3 cup milk
1 (7-oz.) can whole kernel corn
1 teaspoon prepared mustard
1/2 cup shredded Cheddar cheese (2 oz.)
1 tablespoon chopped fresh parsley
Salt and pepper to taste
1 to 2 tablespoons vegetable oil
12 bacon slices
Additional prepared mustard
Sprigs of parsley to garnish

Sift cornmeal and flour into a large bowl. Add eggs and milk and beat to make a smooth batter. Stir in corn, mustard, cheese and parsley. Season with salt and pepper. Heat 1 tablespoon of oil in a large skillet. When hot, add tablespoonfuls of batter mixture. Cook 1 minute, until golden, then turn over and cook on other side. Keep warm while preparing remaining batter, adding additional oil, if neccessary. Preheat broiler. Spread each bacon slice with a thin coat of mustard, roll up and thread onto a metal skewer. Broil 3 to 4 minutes, turning frequently, until golden. Serve fritters with bacon rolls, garnished with sprigs of parsley.

Makes 6 servings.

Corned Beef Hash

1 tablespoon vegetable oil
3 bacon slices
1 onion, chopped
1 pound potatoes, cooked, diced
1 (10-1/2-oz.) can corned beef, diced
1 large egg, beaten
3 tablespoons half and half
2 tablespoons chopped fresh parsley
Salt and pepper to taste
Sprigs of parsley to garnish

Heat oil in a large skillet. Chop bacon finely. Add bacon and onion to oil and cook 2 to 3 minutes. Remove with a slotted spoon, leaving any oil in skillet. In a large bowl, mix bacon, onion, potatoes, corned beef, egg, half and half and parsley. Season with salt and pepper. Spoon into skillet and press down firmly. Cook over medium heat 15 to 20 minutes, until well-browned on bottom. Turn and cook 5 to 10 minutes more. Serve immediately garnished with sprigs of parsley.

Makes 4 to 6 servings.

Kedgeree

12 ounces smoked cod fillets, skinned
8 ounces kipper (herring) fillets, skinned
4-1/2 cups water
1/4 cup wild rice
3/4 cup brown rice
4 tablespoons butter
1 onion, chopped
2 teaspoons curry powder
2 hard-cooked eggs, diced
Juice of 1/2 lemon
2 tablespoons chopped fresh parsley
2/3 cup dairy sour cream
Salt and pepper to taste
Lemon wedges and sprigs of parsley to
    garnish

In a large saucepan, poach fish in 2-1/2 cups of water 10 to 12 minutes, until fish flakes easily. Remove fish with a slotted spoon, reserving cooking liquid, and flake fish. In a medium-size saucepan, combine fish cooking liquid and wild rice. Bring to a boil and simmer 15 minutes. Stir in brown rice and remaining water. Cover and simmer 25 minutes, then drain. In a large skillet, melt butter and sauté onion until slightly softened and transparent. Stir in rice and curry powder and cook 2 to 3 minutes. Stir in flaked fish, eggs, lemon juice, chopped parsley and sour cream and heat through. Season with pepper and salt. Serve garnished with lemon wedges and sprigs of parsley.

Makes 4 servings.

Herb Popovers with Buttered Eggs

Herb Popovers:
3/4 cup all-purpose flour
1/2 teaspoon celery salt
2 large eggs
1 cup milk
1 tablespoon butter, melted
2 tablespoons chopped fresh mixed
**   herbs, such as chervil, parsley, chives**
**   and tarragon**

Buttered Eggs:
1/4 cup butter
6 large eggs, beaten
2 tablespoons chopped fresh mixed
**   herbs, such as chervil, parsley, chives**
**   and tarragon**
2 tablespoons half and half
Salt and pepper to taste

To prepare popovers, generously grease a 12-cup muffin pan. Sift flour and celery salt into a large bowl. Add eggs, milk and butter and beat well. Stir in mixed herbs. Pour mixture into greased muffin cups. Place in cold oven, set temperature at 425F (220C) and bake 30 minutes without opening oven door. To prepare buttered eggs, melt butter in a small saucepan. Add eggs and cook over low heat, stirring constantly, until thickened. Remove from heat and stir in mixed herbs and half and half. Season with salt and pepper. Serve each person 2 popovers with a mound of buttered eggs.

Makes 6 servings.

Orange & Raisin Bread

4 cups bread flour
1 teaspoon sugar
1 teaspoon salt
2 teaspoons apple-pie spice
1 (1/4-oz.) envelope fast-rising yeast
  (about 1 tablespoon)
1 cup milk
4 tablespoons butter
1 large egg, beaten
1/2 cup dark raisins, chopped
Grated peel of 2 oranges
1/4 cup packed light-brown sugar
Beaten egg to glaze

Flavored Butter:
8 tablespoons butter, softened
1/2 teaspoon ground cinnamon
2 teaspoons orange marmalade

Sift flour, sugar, salt and spice into a large bowl. Stir in yeast. In a small saucepan, heat milk and butter to 125F (50C) to 130F (55C). Add 1 beaten egg. Stir into dry ingredients and mix to a firm dough. Knead on a floured surface until smooth and elastic. Clean bowl and oil well. Place dough in oiled bowl. Cover and let stand in a warm place until double in size. Grease a 9" x 5" loaf pan. In a small bowl, mix raisins, orange peel and brown sugar. Knead dough, then roll out in a 20" x 10" rectangle. Sprinkle with raisin filling and roll up from narrow end, jelly-roll style. Pinch together at each end to enclose filling and place in greased loaf pan. Cover and let stand in a warm place until doubled in size. Meanwhile, preheat oven to 425F (220C). Brush dough with beaten egg and bake in preheated oven 30 minutes. Turn out and cool on a wire rack. To prepare flavored butter, in a small bowl, beat butter, cinnamon and marmalade. Spoon into a small serving dish and chill. Serve with warm bread.

Make 1 loaf.

Blueberry Muffins

2 cups bread flour
2 teaspoons baking powder
1/2 teaspoon salt
1/4 cup sugar
2 large eggs, beaten
4 tablespoons butter, melted
3/4 cup milk
1 cup blueberries, drained

Preheat oven to 400F (205C). Grease a 12-cup muffin pan. Sift flour, baking powder, salt and sugar into a large bowl. Make a well in center. Add eggs, butter and milk and mix lightly. Stir in blueberries and spoon into greased muffin cups. Place in oven, lower temperature to 375F (190C) and bake 25 to 30 minutes, until well risen and golden. Remove muffins from cups and cool slightly on a wire rack.

Makes 12 muffins.

Note: Serve warm with jam and cream cheese.

Banana & Raisin Loaf

2 small bananas
4 tablespoons margarine, softened
1 large egg
2/3 cup sugar
Pinch salt
1-1/4 cups self-rising flour
1 teaspoon baking soda
1 tablespoon malt extract or dark
    molasses
1/3 cup golden raisins

Preheat oven to 375F (190C). Grease a 9" x 5" loaf pan. In a blender or food processor fitted with the metal blade, process bananas, margarine, egg, sugar and salt 30 seconds. Add flour, baking soda, malt extract or molasses and process 45 seconds. Stir in raisins. Pour into greased loaf pan and bake in preheated oven 45 minutes. Cool slightly in pan before turning out onto a wire rack.

Makes 1 loaf.

Note: This is best kept for at least a day before serving. Serve thick slices with butter and preserves.

Apple-Cinnamon Waffles

Waffles:
1 cup self-rising flour
1 tablespoon sugar
1/4 teaspoon ground cinnamon
1 large egg, separated
2 tablespoons butter, melted
Grated peel of 1/2 orange
2/3 cup milk

Apple-Cinnamon Topping:
1 pound cooking apples
1/3 cup sugar
Pinch ground cinnamon
1 tablespoon butter
Juice of 1 orange

Plain yogurt to serve

To prepare waffles, in a medium-size bowl, combine flour, sugar and cinnamon. Add egg yolk, butter, orange peel and milk and beat to make a smooth batter. In a small bowl, whisk egg white until it forms stiff peaks, then fold into batter. To prepare topping, peel, core and coarsely chop apples. In a large saucepan, combine apples, sugar, cinnamon, butter and orange juice. Cook over low heat until apples are just soft. Heat an electric waffle iron and brush with oil. Fill with batter, close lid and cook until any steam ceases to escape, about 2 to 3 minutes, and waffles are golden and crisp. Remove and keep warm. Repeat with remaining batter. Serve waffles with topping and yogurt.

Makes 6 servings.

Baked Salmon & Eggs

4 slices smoked salmon
4 large eggs
Salt and pepper to taste
1/4 cup crème frâiche
1 to 2 teaspoons chopped fresh dill
Sprigs of dill to garnish

Preheat oven to 350F (175C). Trim a small 2-inch-long strip from each piece of salmon and reserve. Line 4 ramekins with salmon slices and crack an egg into each one. Season with salt and pepper. In a small bowl, mix crème frâiche and chopped dill and divide equally among ramekins. Place ramekins in a roasting pan half filled with hot water. Bake in preheated oven 15 minutes. Roll reserved salmon strips in small curls and garnish with salmon rolls and sprigs of dill.

Makes 4 servings.

Note: Serve with toast.

Prosciutto with Figs

4 ounces prosciutto, sliced very thin
4 fresh figs
4 fig or vine leaves
1 teaspoon honey
1 tablespoon plus 1 teaspoon fresh lime
   juice
1 tablespoon plus 2 teaspoons olive oil
1 teaspoon pink peppercorns, slightly
   crushed
Shredded lime peel to garnish

Trim any excess fat from prosciutto
and cut in half lengthwise. Cut figs in
quarters. Arrange fig leaves on individual plates and pleat prosciutto on
top. Place figs in prosciutto nest. In a
small bowl, combine honey, lime juice,
olive oil and peppercorns and whisk
well. Spoon over figs and ham and garnish with shredded lime peel.

Makes 4 servings.

Brioche

2 cups bread flour
2 teaspoons sugar
Pinch salt
1 (1/4-oz.) package fast-rising yeast
  (about 1 tablespoon)
3 eggs
1 tablespoon plus 2 teaspoons water
4 tablespoons butter

Sift flour, sugar and salt into a large bowl and stir in yeast. In a small bowl, beat 2 eggs. In a small saucepan, heat water and butter to 125F (50C) to 130F (55C). Add water and butter, the 2 beaten eggs and mix to a soft dough. Turn onto a floured surface and knead 5 minutes. Clean bowl and oil well. Place dough in oiled bowl. Cover and let stand in warm place about 1 hour, until double in size. Meanwhile, generously oil a brioche pan. Shape 3/4 of dough in a ball and push into oiled pan. Shape remaining dough in a ball and place on top, pushing a floured finger through both balls. Cover with oiled plastic and let stand in a warm place until the dough is raised and just to top of pan. Meanwhile, preheat oven to 450F (230C). In a small bowl, beat remaining egg. Brush dough with beaten egg. Bake in preheated oven 10 minutes. Reduce heat to 400F (205C) and bake 10 to 15 minutes, until golden-brown.

Makes 4 to 6 servings.

Note: Serve with butter curls and homemade jam.

Peaches & Cream Toast

2/3 cup half and half
2 eggs
1 tablespoon plus 1 teaspoon peach jam
Few drops vanilla extract
1 (10-inch) French bread loaf
1 tablespoon vegetable oil
1 tablespoon butter
2 fresh peaches
1/4 cup plain yogurt
2 tablespoons toasted hazelnuts

In a medium-size bowl, beat half and half, eggs, 1 tablespoon of jam and vanilla. Slice bread in 1-inch pieces and dip into cream mixture. Heat oil and butter in a large skillet and quickly fry bread until crisp and golden. Slice peaches thinly. In a small bowl, gently combine yogurt and remaining jam. Place 2 slices of toast on each of 4 plates and top with a fan of peach slices. Serve with peach yogurt sprinkled with toasted hazelnuts.

Makes 4 servings.

Oat-Cream Mousse

3 tablespoons regular rolled oats
1-1/4 cups milk
2 tablespoons granulated sugar
1 (1/4-oz.) envelope unflavored gelatin
 (about 1 tablespoon)
2 tablespoons water
1/2 cup plain yogurt
Few drops vanilla extract
1-1/4 cups whipping cream
12 ounces strawberries
3/4 cup raspberries
2 tablespoons powdered sugar

In a medium-size saucepan, combine oats and milk. Bring to a boil, stirring continuously, then simmer 3 minutes. Remove from heat. Stir in granulated sugar and cool. In a small bowl, sprinkle gelatin over water. Let stand 2 to 3 minutes, until softened. Set bowl of gelatin in a saucepan of hot water and stir until dissolved and quite hot. Remove bowl from pan and cool. Stir gelatin, yogurt and vanilla into oat mixture. In a medium-size bowl, whip cream until stiff, then fold into oat mixture. Pour into a ring mold and chill until set. To serve, unmold mousse on a serving plate and fill center with strawberries. Sieve raspberries into a small bowl and stir in powdered sugar. Pour raspberry puree over strawberries and serve at once.

Makes 6 servings.

Peach Melba Hearts

1/3 cup plain yogurt
1-1/4 cups fromage frais or ricotta cheese
1/3 cup whipping cream
1 tablespoon plus 1 to 2 teaspoons sugar
Few drops vanilla extract
2 peaches, peeled, pitted
1 cup raspberries
Additional sugar to taste
Mint leaves and additional raspberries to
   garnish

Wet 4 squares of muslin and wring out until just damp. Line 4 coeurs à la crème molds with muslin. In a large bowl, whisk yogurt, fromage frais or ricotta cheese, whipping cream, 1 tablespoon plus 1 to 2 teaspoons sugar and vanilla until thick. Spoon into prepared molds and tap gently to level surface. Fold over any excess muslin and place molds on a wire rack set over a bowl. Chill at least 4 hours or overnight for mixture to drain. In a blender or food processor fitted with the metal blade, blend peaches and 1 cup raspberries until smooth. Sieve fruit puree to remove any skin and seeds and sweeten to taste with additional sugar. Unwrap hearts and turn out onto individual plates. Peel off muslin and pour fruit sauce over hearts. Garnish each with a sprig of mint and a few raspberries.

Makes 4 servings.

Melon Sorbet

1 Galia melon
1/3 cup sugar
2/3 cup water
1 (1-inch) piece gingerroot, thinly sliced
1/4 cup ginger wine, Madeira or sweet
   sherry
2 tablespoons orange juice
2 tablespoons lemon juice
Raddichio leaves
Stem ginger, cut in thin strips, and
   sprigs of chervil to garnish

Cut melon in half and remove seeds. Scoop out pulp. In a blender or food processor fitted with the metal blade, process pulp to a puree. In a small saucepan, combine sugar, water and gingerroot and bring slowly to a boil, stirring constantly. Simmer 3 minutes, then remove from heat and cool. Stir in melon puree, ginger wine, Madeira or sweet sherry, and orange and lemon juices. Strain into a plastic container or freezer tray, cover and freeze 2 to 3 hours. When sorbet is nearly frozen and slushly, blend or process again until softened and pale. Return to freezer to firm up. Serve scoops of sorbet on raddichio leaves garnished with stem ginger and sprigs of chervil.

Makes 6 to 8 servings.

Tomato & Basil Sorbet

4 large fresh tomatoes
1 (8-oz.) can ready-cut tomatoes
1 teaspoon sugar
2 teaspoons tomato paste
2 teaspoons wine vinegar
1/2 teaspoon onion salt
1 teaspoon Worcestershire sauce
2 teaspoons chopped fresh basil
1 tablespoon plus 1 teaspoon vodka

Remove tops from fresh tomatoes and scoop out all seeds and flesh, leaving 4 shells. Place shells and tops in freezer. In a blender or food processor fitted with the metal blade, process tomato flesh and seeds and remaining ingredients 2 minutes. Pour into a plastic container and freeze. When frozen to a slush, process in blender or food processor until slightly softened and pale. Using a pastry bag fitted with a plain nozzle, pipe sorbet into frozen shells. Return to freezer until firm.

Makes 4 servings.

Note: Serve with hot buttered toast.

Christmas Omelet

3 eggs, separated, plus 1 extra white
1 tablespoon plus 2 teaspoons sugar
Few drops vanilla extract
1 tablespoon butter
2 tablespoons mincemeat
1 to 2 teaspoons brandy, if desired
Powdered sugar

Preheat oven to 350F (175C). In a large bowl, beat egg yolks, sugar and vanilla until light and creamy. In a medium-size bowl, whisk egg whites until stiff and fold gently into yolk mixture. Pour egg mixture into a skillet and cook over low heat 1 minute. Bake in preheated oven 7 minutes, until just set. In a small bowl, mix mincemeat and brandy, if desired, and spread over omelet. Fold omelet in half and slide onto a warmed plate. Dust with powdered sugar and mark with a hot skewer, if desired. Serve immediately.

Makes 2 servings.

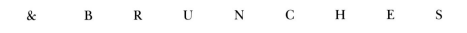

—— Avocado & Camembert Omelet ——

4 large eggs
2 tablespoons grated Parmesan cheese
2 tablespoons butter
1 small avocado
1 tablespoon dairy sour cream
Pinch of ground nutmeg
Salt and pepper to taste
2 ounces Camembert cheese, diced
Sprigs of parsley to garnish

In a large bowl, beat eggs and Parmesan cheese. In a large skillet, melt 1/2 of butter and pour in 1/2 of egg mixture. Cook until set. Prepare remaining omelet in same way. Cut avocado in half and discard pit. Slice 1 avocado half thinly in long fingers. In a small bowl, mash remaining half. Stir in sour cream and nutmeg. Season with salt and pepper. Stir in camembert cheese. Arrange 1/2 of avocado fingers in a fan shape on top of each omelet and top each with 1/2 of camembert mixture. Broil 1 minute, until cheese melts. Fold omelets in half and place on warmed plates. Garnish with sprigs of parsley and serve immediately.

Makes 2 servings.

Eggs & Oysters

4 crumpets or English muffins
4 tablespoons butter
6 eggs, beaten
Salt and pepper to taste
1 (3-3/4-oz.) can smoked oysters
1 tablespoon chopped fresh chives

Toast crumpets or muffins and keep warm. Melt butter over low heat in a small skillet. Add eggs and season with salt and pepper. Stir constantly until eggs thicken. Drain oysters and stir into eggs. Stir in chives and cook until oysters are warmed through. Spoon mixture on top of crumpets or muffins and serve immediately.

Makes 4 servings.

Trout Quenelles

2 large trout, skinned, filleted
1 egg, separated
2 teaspoons chopped fresh dill
1 tablespoon dairy sour cream
Salt and pepper to taste
Pinch ground nutmeg
2 cups fish stock
1 tablespoon lemon juice
1/2 cucumber, grated
1/2 cup whipping cream
1/2 teaspoon cornstarch
Cucumber and lemon twists and sprigs
    of dill to garnish

In a blender or food processor fitted with the metal blade, process trout, egg white, chopped dill, sour cream and salt and pepper 30 seconds. Pour fish stock and lemon juice into a medium-size saucepan and bring to a boil. Reduce heat, until stock is just simmering. Using 2 small spoons, shape trout mixture in 8 ovals and drop into stock. Poach 3 to 4 minutes, until quenelles rise to top of poaching liquid. Remove with a slotted spoon and keep warm. Reduce poaching liquid to 2/3 cup. Add cucumber and boil 5 minutes more until grated cucumber is tender. In blender or food processor, process cucumber mixture until smooth. In a small bowl, mix egg yolk and whipping cream and pour a small amount of cucumber sauce on top. Mix well, then return to pan with remainder of cucumber sauce. Heat gently, stirring constantly, until slightly thickened. Pour sauce on 4 warmed plates and arrange trout quenelles on top. Garnish with twists of lemon and cucumber and sprigs of dill.

Makes 4 servings.

Winter Compote

1 cup dried figs, quartered
1 cup dried prunes
1 cup dried apricots
1/2 cup cranberries, thawed if frozen
2/3 cup port
2/3 cup prepared China tea
2/3 cup water
Pared peel and juice of 1/2 lemon
1 cup ricotta cheese
1 to 2 teaspoons honey
1/4 cup toasted sliced almonds to
    decorate

In a large saucepan, combine dried fruits, cranberries, port, tea, water and lemon peel. Bring slowly to a boil. Cover and simmer 20 minutes. Remove from heat and cool. When completely cold, stir in lemon juice to taste. Chill 2 hours. In a small bowl, beat 2 teaspoons of compote juice, ricotta cheese and honey to taste. Spoon compote into individual dishes and top with a spoonful of cheese mixture. Decorate with toasted almonds.

Makes 4 to 6 servings.

Grilled Citrus Cocktail

2 pink grapefruit
1 white grapefruit
3 oranges
1 lime
1 tablespoon plus 1 teaspoon sweet
   sherry
2 tablespoons plus 2 teaspoons
   light-brown sugar
1 tablespoon plus 1 teaspoon butter
Sprigs of lemon balm to garnish

Cut grapefruts in half and, using a
grapefruit knife, remove pulp and cut
in sections. Reserve 4 grapefruit shells.
Cut away top and bottom from oranges
and lime, then remove all skin and pith.
Cut in sections, reserving any juices. In
a large bowl, mix grapefruit, orange
and lime sections. Arrange fruit in
grapefruit shells and sprinkle 1 teaspoon of sherry over each. Sprinkle
with brown sugar and top with 1 teaspoon of butter. Broil until brown
sugar melts. Top with reserved fruit
juices and serve immediately garnished
with sprigs of lemon balm.

Makes 4 servings.

Trout Rolls

4 large trout, filleted
Salt and pepper to taste
8 large sprigs tarragon
1 red onion, sliced in rings
1/2 cup raspberry vinegar
1-1/2 cups water
3 bay leaves
Sprigs of fennel

Preheat oven to 350F (175C). Place fish fillets skin-side down on a flat surface and season well with salt and pepper. Place 1 sprig of tarragon at 1 end of each fillet and roll up, jelly-roll style. Pack rolls tightly in a shallow ovenproof dish and cover with onion rings. In a small bowl, mix vinegar and water and pour over fish. Add bay leaves and sprigs of fennel and cover with foil. Bake in preheated oven 25 minutes. Cool in cooking liquid.

Makes 4 servings.

Note: Serve with slices of whole-wheat bread and butter.

Quick Blinis

1/2 cup bread flour
1/2 cup buckwheat flour
1 teaspoon salt
1/3 (1/4-oz.) envelope fast-rising yeast
   (1 teaspoon)
1 cup milk
1 egg, separated
1 tablespoon butter
1 tablespoon vegetable oil
1-1/4 cups dairy sour cream

Sift flours and salt into a large bowl and stir in yeast. In a small saucepan, heat milk to 125F (50C) to 130F (55C). Stir egg yolk into warm milk, then blend milk mixture into flour to make a thick batter. Cover and let stand in a warm place 1 hour, until double in size. In a small bowl, whisk egg white until stiff and fold into batter. Cover and let stand in a warm place 45 minutes. Melt a small amount of butter and some of oil on a griddle. Pour in large spoonfuls of batter and cook 1 to 2 minutes, until holes appear on surface. Turn over and cook other side; keep warm. Repeat with remaining butter, oil and batter. Serve topped with spoonfuls of sour cream.

Makes 12 servings.

Note: If desired, serve with mixed fish roe and sprigs of dill.

—————— Gingered Fruit Salad ——————

1 large pineapple
2 oranges, peeled, sectioned
3/4 cup strawberries, hulled
1/2 cup seedless green grapes
2 kiwifruit, peeled, sliced
1 starfruit, thinly sliced
1/4 cup water
1/4 cup sugar
1 (1-inch) piece gingerroot, thinly sliced
Pared peel and juice of 1 lime

Cut pineapple in half. Using a grapefruit knife, remove pulp leaving shells intact. Discard hard core from pineapple and cut pulp in large chunks. In a large bowl, mix pineapple, oranges, strawberries, grapes, kiwifruit and starfruit and any fruit juices. In a small pan, mix water and sugar. Add gingerroot, 1/2 of lime peel and all lime juice to syrup. Bring slowly to a boil, stirring constantly. Simmer 1 minute, then remove ginger and lime peel. Cut remaining lime peel in julienne strips and add to syrup. Simmer 1 minute, then remove and cool. Pile fruit into reserved pineapple shells and pour ginger syrup over fruit. Sprinkle with lime strips and chill.

Makes 4 to 6 servings.

Maple Crunch Cereal

2 cups regular rolled oats
4-1/4 cups wheat flakes
1/3 cup shredded unsweetened coconut
1 tablespoon sesame seeds
1/3 cup sunflower seeds
1/2 cup hazelnuts, chopped
1/2 cup Brazil nuts, chopped
1/3 cup maple syrup
1/3 cup sunflower oil
Few drops vanilla extract

Preheat oven to 250F (120C). In a large bowl, mix oats, wheat flakes, coconut, sesame seeds, sunflower seeds, hazelnuts and Brazil nuts. In a small pan, heat syrup and sunflower oil. Pour over dry ingredients and mix well. Spread mixture on a large shallow baking sheet and bake in preheated oven 1 hour, turning frequently, until toasted all over. Cool and store in a large airtight container.

Makes 4 servings.

Note: Serve with fresh fruit, plain yogurt and honey.

Pink Grapefruit Sorbet

3/4 cup sugar
1-1/4 cups water
2/3 (1/4-oz.) envelope unflavored gelatin
(2 teaspoons)
3 pink grapefruit
Sprigs of mint to garnish

In a small saucepan, combine sugar and water. Sprinkle gelatin over liquid and let stand 5 minutes, until softened. Cook over low heat, stirring constantly, until sugar and gelatin dissolve. Remove from heat and cool. Cut grapefruits in half and, using a spoon, remove all pulp, leaving shells intact. Scallop edges of grapefruit shells and freeze. In a blender or food processor fitted with the metal blade, process pulp to a puree. Stir puree into syrup. Pour into a plastic freezer container and freeze 1 to 2 hours, until just frozen. Blend or process sorbet or whisk until soft and pale, then return to freezer 2 to 3 hours, until firm. Serve scoops of sorbet in frozen grapefruit shells garnished with sprigs of mint.

Makes 6 servings.

Chewy Fruit Bars

1/2 cup dried figs
3/4 cup dried apricots
3/4 cup dried pears
2/3 cup dried dates
1/2 cup sunflower seeds
1/2 cup roasted hazelnuts, chopped
1/2 cup regular rolled oats
1/2 cup whole-wheat flour
1 egg, beaten
1/4 cup apple juice
1 ounce carob

Preheat oven to 325F (165C). Line a jelly-roll pan with parchment paper. In a blender or food processor fitted with the metal blade, process dried fruits until finely chopped. Stir in sunflower seeds, hazelnuts, oats and flour and mix well. Stir in egg and apple juice. Turn into prepared pan and bake in preheated oven 25 to 30 minutes. Cool slightly in pan. Turn out and cut in bars. Melt carob in the top of a double boiler or a bowl set over a pan of simmering water. Using a pastry bag fitted with a plain nozzle, pipe melted carob in a lattice over top of bars. Let stand until carob sets. Store in a large airtight container.

Makes 24 bars.

Herb Baked Eggs

4 thin slices ham
3 large eggs
1 teaspoon prepared mustard
1/4 cup plain yogurt
3/4 cup shredded Cheddar cheese (3 oz.)
2 teaspoon chopped fresh chives
2 teaspoons chopped fresh parsley
Sprigs of herbs to garnish

Preheat oven to 375F (190C). Grease 4 ramekins. Line greased ramekins with ham slices. In a medium-size bowl, beat eggs, mustard and yogurt. Stir 1/4 cup of cheese into egg mixture. In a small bowl, mix chives and parsley and add 1/2 of mixed herbs to egg mixture. Stir well, then spoon into prepared ramekins. Sprinkle with remaining cheese and herbs. Bake in preheated oven 25 to 30 minutes, until golden and set. Turn out onto serving plates and garnish with sprigs of herbs.

Makes 4 servings.

Note: Serve with hot buttered toast.

Sausage-Stuffed Mushrooms

6 large flat mushrooms
1 tablespoon vegetable oil
12 ounces pork sausage
1 (8-oz.) can ready-cut tomatoes, drained
2 teaspoons tomato paste
2 teaspoons chopped sweet pickle
Salt and pepper to taste
4 ounces thinly sliced mozzarella cheese
Sprigs of basil to garnish

Preheat broiler. Place mushrooms on a baking sheet. Brush tops of mushrooms with oil. Broil mushrooms 1 minute. In a medium-size skillet, fry sausage 3 minutes, stirring to break up sausage. Stir in drained tomatoes, tomato paste and chopped sweet pickle. Bring to a boil and cook until thickened, stirring frequently. Season with salt and pepper. Spoon filling into mushrooms. Top with cheese and broil until cheese is bubbly. Serve at once, garnished with sprigs of basil.

Makes 6 servings.

Fruit Brochettes

1 nectarine, cubed
4 apricots, halved
8 strawberries
1 peach, cubed
4 plums, quartered
1 tablespoon honey
1 teaspoon finely grated lemon peel
2 teaspoons lemon juice
Pinch grated nutmeg
2 passion fruit
3/4 cup fromage frais or ricotta cheese

Thread nectarine, apricots, strawberries, peach and plums onto skewers. In a small bowl, mix honey, lemon peel and juice and nutmeg; brush over fruit. Broil 2 minutes, turning brochettes over after 1 minute. Halve passion fruit and scoop out seeds and juice with a teaspoon. Mix with the fromage frais or ricotta cheese and serve with hot fruit brochettes.

Makes 4 servings.

Mixed Melon Salad

1 honeydew melon
1 cantaloupe
1/4 watermelon
1/2 cup seedless green grapes
1 tablespoon superfine sugar
1 tablespoon tarragon vinegar
2 tablespoons vegetable oil
2 teaspoons chopped fresh mint
1 teaspoon chopped fresh tarragon
2 slightly firm avocados
Sprigs of mint and chervil to garnish

Cut honeydew melon and cantaloupe in half and remove seeds. Remove seeds from watermelon. Using a melon baller, scoop out melon balls; place in a large serving bowl and add grapes. In a small bowl, mix sugar, vinegar and oil and pour over fruit. Stir in chopped herbs. Cover and chill 1 hour. Cut avocados in half and remove pits. Using melon baller, scoop out pulp and add to fruit; mix well. Garnish with sprigs of mint and chervil.

Makes 4 servings.

Banana Crunch

Juice of 1/2 lemon
4 small bananas
1/4 cup banana yogurt
1 cup fromage frais or ricotta cheese
1 egg white
1/4 cup Maple Crunch Cereal, page 45

Pour lemon juice into a small bowl. Slice bananas thickly and toss in lemon juice. In another small bowl, mix banana yogurt and fromage frais or cottage cheese. In another small bowl, whisk egg white until it forms stiff peaks and fold into yogurt mixture. In dessert dishes, layer bananas and yogurt mixture and top each with 1 tablespoon of cereal. Serve at once.

Makes 4 servings.

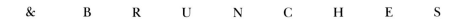

Watermelon & Apple Slush

1/2 large watermelon
2-1/2 cups apple juice
6 to 12 teaspoons mint syrup
Sprigs of mint and thin apple slices to
    garnish

Scoop pulp from watermelon and re-move any seeds. In a blender or food processor fitted with the metal blade, process pulp until smooth. Pour into a shallow freezer container and mix in 1-1/4 cups of apple juice. Freeze until slushy. Remove and whisk to break up ice crystals. Return to freezer and freeze until firm. To serve, refrigerate sorbet 20 minutes. Using a knife, coarsely chop sorbet and spoon into tall glasses. Pour remaining apple juice equally among glasses and top with 1 to 2 teaspoonfuls of mint syrup. Garnish with sprigs of mint and apple slices.

Makes 6 servings.

Variation: Substitute creme de menthe for mint syrup.

Sausage & Bean Rolls

6 crusty white rolls
4 tablespoons butter, melted
8 ounces Dutch pork smoked sausage
1 small onion, finely chopped
1 (16-oz.) can baked beans
Sprigs of watercress to garnish

Preheat oven to 400F (205C). Cut tops off rolls and set aside. Hollow out and discard centers of rolls, leaving a thin wall of bread. Brush insides of rolls with 3/4 of butter. Wrap foil around each roll, leaving top open. Place on a baking sheet and bake in preheated oven 10 minutes. In a medium-size saucepan, simmer sausage in boiling water 10 minutes. In a medium-size skillet, sauté onion in remaining butter until slightly softened and transparent. Cut sausage in thin slices. Stir into onion, add baked beans and heat through. Remove foil from rolls and spoon in sausage mixture. Replace bread tops and return to oven 2 to 3 minutes more. Serve at once, garnished with watercress.

Makes 6 servings.

Soufflé-Filled Tomatoes

4 medium-size tomatoes
Salt and pepper to taste
4 (1-inch-thick) slices white bread
1/3 cup garlic-herb butter, see note
1 (6-oz.) can tuna, drained
2 tablespoons fresh bread crumbs
1 teaspoon pesto sauce
1 egg, separated
1 teaspoon grated Parmesan cheese
Sprigs of basil to garnish

Cut tops off tomatoes and remove seeds and pulp. Reserve tomato pulp for another use. Season insides of tomatoes with salt and pepper. Turn upside down on paper towels to drain. Remove crusts from bread, and using a 2-inch cookie cutter, cut holes in center of each slice. Prepare 2 tablespoons of bread crumbs from bread holes. In a small saucepan, melt 1/4 cup of garlic-herb butter and brush over both sides of each slice of bread. Place bread on a baking sheet and set aside. Preheat oven to 400F (205C). In a small saucepan, melt remaining butter and stir in bread crumbs, tuna and pesto sauce. In a small bowl, whisk egg white until stiff.

Stir egg yolk into tuna mixture and fold in egg white. Set tomatoes in holes in bread and fill with tuna mixture. Sprinkle with Parmesan cheese and bake in preheated oven 12 to 15 minutes, until soufflé is well risen and golden and bread is crisp. Garnish with sprigs of basil and serve immediately.

Makes 4 servings.

Note: To prepare garlic-herb butter, flavor 1/3 cup softened butter with crushed garlic and chopped fresh herbs to taste.

Scotch Woodcock

4 slices whole-wheat bread
4 tablespoons butter
1 teaspoon anchovy paste
2 teaspoons water
1 (2-oz.) can anchovies
3 tablespoons milk
2 large eggs
Pinch paprika
Sprigs of parsley

Toast bread and remove crusts. Butter toast. In a small bowl, combine anchovy paste and water and spread thinly on buttered toast. In a small saucepan, melt remaining butter. Drain anchovies and measure 2 teaspoons anchovy oil. In a small bowl, whisk anchovy oil, milk and eggs. Pour into butter and cook over low heat, stirring constantly, until mixture thickens. Spread on top of pre-pared toast and cut in triangles. Criss-cross with thin strips of anchovy fillets and sprinkle with paprika. Serve im-mediately, garnished with sprigs of parsley.

Makes 4 servings.

Sunday Treats

4 bagels
1/2 cup cream cheese, softened
2 teaspoons half and half
2 teaspoons capers, chopped
4 small gherkin pickles, finely chopped
1 teaspoon finely chopped fresh dill
2 ounces smoked salmon
Freshly ground pepper
Lemon wedges to serve

Cut bagels in half. In a small bowl, beat cream cheese and half and half. Stir in capers, pickles and dill. Spread generously over both sides of each bagel and arrange 1/2 ounce of smoked salmon on top. Sprinkle with pepper and serve with lemon wedges.

Makes 4 servings.

Coulibiac

3 tablespoons butter
1 onion, diced
1 cup button mushrooms, sliced
1/4 cup plus 2 tablespoons cooked white
  long-grain rice
2 tablespoons chopped fresh parsley
Salt and pepper to taste
12 ounces fresh salmon fillet
3/4 cup dry white wine
1/2 cup water
1 egg, hard-cooked
1 (17-1/4-oz.) package frozen puff pastry,
  thawed
1 egg, beaten
1-1/4 cups dairy sour cream, if desired
Lemon twists and sprigs of dill to
  garnish

In a large skillet, melt butter and gently
sauté onions until slightly softened and
transparent. Add mushrooms and cook
5 minutes more. Remove from heat
and stir in rice and parsley. Season with
salt and pepper and cool. Place salmon
in a shallow saucepan. Pour on wine
and water and simmer 10 minutes, until just cooked. Remove salmon with a

slotted spoon and flake. Chop hard-
cooked egg in small pieces. Roll out 3/4
of pastry in 15" x 10" rectangle and
brush with beaten egg. Arrange 1/2 of
mushroom mixture down center third
of pastry, leaving a 2-1/2-inch strip on
top and bottom. Top with 1/2 of flaked
salmon, then chopped egg. Cover with
remaining salmon and mushroom mixture. Fold sides of pastry up and over
top of filling so that the edges overlap;
fold ends over top. Brush with beaten
egg to seal. Turn over and place couli-
biac on a baking sheet with the sealed
edges underneath. Preheat oven to
425F (220C). Roll out remaining pastry
and cut out fish shapes. Brush pastry all
over with egg. Make a small hole in top
and decorate with fish shapes. Bake in
preheated oven 25 minutes, until pastry is golden. Serve in thick slices with
sour cream, if desired, garnished with
lemon twists and sprigs of dill.

Makes 6 to 8 servings.

—— Hash Browns with Tomato Relish ——

1-1/2 pounds boiling potatoes
6 bacon slices
Salt and pepper to taste
3 tablespoons butter
2 tablespoons vegetable oil
1 onion, finely chopped
1 (8-oz.) can ready-cut tomatoes
2 teaspoons tomato paste
1/2 teaspoons sugar
1 teaspoon prepared horseradish
1 teaspoon prepared mustard
1/2 teaspoon chopped fresh thyme

Place potatoes in a large saucepan of boiling salted water. Bring to a boil and simmer 10 minutes. Drain and cool under cold running water, then pat dry. Chop bacon in very small pieces. Coarsely grate cooked potatoes. In a large bowl, combine potatoes and bacon. Season with salt and pepper. In a large skillet, melt butter and 1 tablespoon of oil. Cook spoonfuls of potato mixture over medium heat until golden and crisp. Turn over and cook other side. Drain on paper towels and keep warm. To prepare tomato relish, in a medium-size saucepan, heat remaining oil and sauté onion until slightly softened. Add tomatoes, tomato paste and sugar. Season with salt and pepper. Cook until thick and pulpy. Stir in horseradish, mustard and thyme and cook 1 minute. Serve hash browns with tomato relish.

Makes 4 servings.

Buck Rarebit

1 cup shredded Cheddar cheese (4 oz.)
1 tablespoon butter
1/2 teaspoon dry mustard powder
2 tablespoons beer
Salt and pepper to taste
3 whole-wheat English muffins, split,
  toasted
6 eggs
3 tablespoons mayonnaise
3 tablespoons chopped watercress
Sprigs of watercress to garnish

In a small saucepan, place cheese, butter, dry mustard and beer. Season with salt and pepper. Heat gently, stirring constantly, until mixture is a creamy sauce. Cool slightly. Preheat broiler. Pour sauce onto toasted muffins and broil until golden and bubbly. Meanwhile, poach eggs in water. Drain, using a slotted spoon, and place on top of each muffin half. In a blender or food processor fitted with the metal blade, blend mayonnaise and chopped watercress until smooth. Top each egg with a spoonful of herbed mayonnaise. Serve immediately, garnished with sprigs of watercress.

Makes 6 servings.

Potato Waffles with Mushrooms

3/4 cup mashed potatoes
1/4 cup hot milk
2 tablespoons all-purpose flour
2 tablespoons butter, melted
Celery salt and pepper to taste
2 eggs, beaten

Mushroom Topping:
3 tablespoons butter
6 green onions, chopped
12 ounces mushrooms, sliced
1-1/4 cups dairy sour cream
1 tablespoon chopped fresh parsley

Chopped chives to garnish

In a medium-size bowl, beat potatoes, hot milk, flour and butter until smooth; season with celery salt and pepper. Add eggs and mix well. Heat an electric waffle iron and brush with oil. Fill one half with potato batter, close and cook until steam ceases to escape, about 2 to 3 minutes, and waffles are golden and crisp. Keep warm. Repeat with remaining batter. To prepare topping, in a large skillet, melt butter and sauté green onions and mushrooms until slightly softened. Add sour cream and heat, stirring constantly until thick. Stir in parsley. To serve, pour topping over waffles and garnish with chopped chives.

Makes 4 servings.

Deviled Kidneys

6 lamb's kidneys
1/4 cup butter
2 teaspoons prepared English mustard
2 teaspoons Worcestershire sauce
1/2 teaspoon red wine vinegar
1 teaspoon tomato paste
Pinch salt
Pinch light-brown sugar
Large pinch red pepper (cayenne)
4 crumpets or English muffins, toasted
1 teaspoon chopped fresh parsley to
    garnish

Cut kidneys in half. Remove skin and
cores and cut each half in 3 or 4 pieces.
In a large saucepan, melt butter and
quickly sauté kidneys 1 to 2 minutes.
Remove kidneys from pan with a slotted spoon. Add mustard, Worcestershire sauce, wine vinegar, tomato paste,
salt, brown sugar and red pepper. Stir
until thick and bubbly. Remove from
heat and stir in kidneys. Spoon mixture
onto toasted crumpets or English muffins. Sprinkle with chopped parsley and
serve at once.

Makes 4 servings.

Croque-Monsieur

4 tablespoons butter
8 slices thick whole-wheat bread
4 thin slices smoked ham
4 thin slices Gruyère cheese
4 to 5 tablespoons vegetable oil
Sprigs of parsley to garnish

Butter bread and top 4 slices with smoked ham, then cheese. Cover with remaining slices of bread and press down well. Using a cutter, cut shapes from sandwiches. Heat oil in a large skillet and quickly fry sandwiches on both sides, until golden-brown. Drain on paper towels. Garnish with sprigs of parsley and serve at once.

Makes 4 servings.

Lemon-Raisin Drop Scones

1 cup self-rising flour
Pinch salt
1 tablespoon sugar
Grated peel and juice 1/2 lemon
3 tablespoons golden raisins
1 egg, beaten
2/3 cup milk
1 tablespoon vegetable oil

Sift flour, salt and sugar into a medium-size bowl. Stir in lemon peel. In a small saucepan, combine lemon juice and raisins and heat gently 3 minutes. Make a well in center of flour mixture and add egg and milk. Beat well to make a smooth batter. Drain raisins and stir into batter. Heat a griddle and brush surface with oil. Pour small rounds of batter onto griddle, spacing well apart from each other. Cook until surface is golden and bubbly. Turn scones over and cook 1 minute more, until other side is golden. Keep warm while preparing remaining scones.

Makes 18 scones.

Note: Serve with butter and ginger preserves.

— Banana & Strawberry Drop Scones —

1 banana
2 cups self-rising flour
2 pinches salt
1 tablespoon plus 1 teaspoon sugar
2 eggs
2/3 cup milk
3/4 cup strawberries, hulled

To Serve:
2 large bananas
1-3/4 cups strawberries, hulled
2 teaspoons lemon juice
Powdered sugar
Butter curls, if desired

In a blender or food processor fitted with the metal blade, process banana, 1 cup of flour, 1 pinch of salt, 2 teaspoons of sugar, 1 egg and 1/3 cup of milk and process to a smooth batter. Pour into a bowl and repeat procedure using strawberries and remaining flour, salt, sugar, egg and milk. Lightly oil a griddle and heat gently. Pour spoonfuls of banana and strawberry batter onto griddle, spacing well apart, and cook until surface is golden and bubbly. Turn over and cook on other side 1 minute. Keep warm while preparing remaining scones. To serve, thinly slice bananas and strawberries and sprinkle with lemon juice. Place 2 drop scones of each flavor on individual serving plates and top with fruit mixture. Dust with powdered sugar and serve with butter curls, if desired.

Makes 5 servings.

Apple-Cinnamon Toasts

1 large baking apple, peeled, cored,
   diced
3 tablespoons butter
1 teaspoon lemon juice
2 teaspoons ground cinnamon
1 tablespoon plus 1 teaspoon light-brown
   sugar
4 large slices bread

In a small saucepan, combine apple,
butter and lemon juice. Cook gently,
until apple is pulpy. Remove from heat
and cool completely. Preheat broiler.
In a small bowl, mix cinnamon and
brown sugar. Toast bread and remove
crusts. Spread bread generously with
apple butter and sprinkle with brown
sugar mixture. Broil until brown sugar
begins to melt. Cut in triangles and
serve at once.

Makes 4 servings.

Apricot & Almond Muffins

1-1/2 cups bread flour
1/4 cup ground almonds
2 teaspoons baking powder
1/2 teaspoon salt
1/4 cup sugar
2 large eggs, beaten
4 tablespoons butter, melted
3/4 cup milk
1 cup dried apricots, finely chopped
1 teaspoon lemon juice
1/4 cup sliced almonds

Preheat oven to 400F (205C). Grease a 12-cup muffin pan. Sift flour, ground almonds, baking powder, salt and sugar into a large bowl. Make a well in center and add eggs, butter and milk and mix lightly. Stir in chopped apricots and lemon juice. Spoon into greased muffin cups. Sprinkle with sliced almonds. Place pan in preheated oven. Reduce temperature to 375F (190C) and bake 25 to 30 minutes, until well risen and golden. Remove muffins from cups and cool slightly on a wire rack.

Makes 12 muffins.

Crunchy Fruit Salad

1/4 cup sugar
3/4 cup water
Pared peel of 1 lime
1 pound strawberries, hulled, sliced
6 kiwifruit, peeled, sliced
**6 passion fruit, halved, seeded, pulp
    removed and chopped**
4 ounces seedless grapes, halved
Freshly chopped mint
Juice of 1/2 lime

In a small saucepan, combine sugar, water and lime peel. Heat gently, stirring constantly, until sugar dissolves. Bring to a boil and boil 2 to 3 minutes. Remove from heat and cool. In a medium-size bowl, mix fruits and sprinkle with chopped mint. Pour in syrup and lime juice and stir gently.

Makes 4 servings.

Note: Serve with buttery shortbread cookies.

Zabaglione Baked Apples

4 large baking apples
1/2 cup sliced almonds
1/3 cup dark raisins
1/2 cup dried apricots, chopped
Grated peel and juice of 1 lemon
1 tablespoon plus 1 teaspoon butter

Zabaglione:
2 egg yolks
2 tablespoons honey
2 tablespoons plus 2 teaspoons Marsala
  wine

Preheat oven to 350F (175C). Wash apples and core. In a small bowl, mix almonds, raisins, apricots and lemon peel. Make a shallow cut in skin around middle of each apple. Place apples in an ovenproof dish. Fill cavities with fruit mixture and pour lemon juice over fruit mixture. Top each apple with 1 teaspoon of butter. Bake in preheated oven 35 minutes. To prepare zabaglione, combine egg yolks, honey and wine in top of a double boiler or a bowl set over a pan of simmering water. Whisk constantly 7 to 10 minutes, until thick and fluffy. To serve, top apples with spoonfuls of zabaglione.

Makes 4 servings.

Strudel Triangles

5 ounces cooked chicken, finely chopped
3/4 cup crumbled feta cheese (3 oz.)
1 small avocado, chopped
2 teaspoons creamed horseradish
Salt and pepper to taste
6 sheets filo pastry, thawed if frozen
5-1/2 tablespoons butter, melted
Sprigs of cilantro to garnish

Preheat oven to 425F (220C). In a medium-size bowl, combine chicken, feta cheese, avocado and horseradish. Season with salt and pepper. Brush 3 sheets of filo pastry with melted butter and lay a second sheet on top of each. Cut each double sheet in 6 (3-inch-wide) strips. Place 1 teaspoon of chicken filling on top corner of each strip and brush pastry with butter. Fold pastry and filling over at right angles to make a triangle and continue folding in this way along strip of pastry to form a triangular bundle. Brush with butter and place on a baking sheet. Repeat with remaining strips. Bake in pre-heated oven 10 to 15 minutes, until golden-brown. Serve warm, garnished with sprigs of cilantro.

Makes 18 triangles.

Shrimp & Mushroom Barquettes

1 cup all-purpose flour
Pinch salt
1 tablespoon grated Parmesan cheese
8-1/2 tablespoons butter, softened
1 egg yolk
1 tablespoon plus 1 teaspoon water
6 ounces button mushrooms, thinly
    sliced (about 1-1/2 cups)
2/3 cup dairy sour cream
1 to 2 teaspoons dry sherry
3 ounces cooked peeled shrimp, chopped
2 to 3 teaspoons chopped fresh chives
Cooked whole shrimp and triangles of
    lemon to garnish

In a food processor fitted with the metal blade, process flour, salt, Parmesan cheese and 5-1/2 tablespoons of butter 30 seconds. Add egg yolk and water and process until mixture binds together. Wrap in plastic wrap and chill 20 minutes. Preheat oven to 425F (220C). On a lightly floured surface, roll out pastry until very thin. Using a rolling pin, lift pastry and lay over barquette pans. Press down lightly and roll rolling pin over pans to trim off excess dough.

Press pastry down in pans. Prick bottom of each pastry shell and stack on top of each other, three pans high. Top with an empty barquette pan. Bake in preheated oven 15 minutes. Remove from oven and unstack pans. Place pans on baking sheets in a single layer. Return to oven 2 to 3 minutes, until crisp. Cool. In a small saucepan, melt remaining butter and gently sauté mushrooms 1 minute. Stir in sour cream and bring to a boil, stirring constantly until thickened. Add sherry, shrimp and chives and mix well. Cool slightly, then spoon into pastry shells. Garnish with whole shrimp and triangles of lemon.

Makes 12 barquettes.

Note: Barquette pans are small boat-shaped pastry pans.

Barbecue Beans & Bacon

1-1/4 cups dried navy beans
Water
2 tablespoons light-brown sugar
1 teaspoon salt
1 tablespoon plus 1 teaspoon dark
   molasses
1 tablespoon plus 1 teaspoon red wine
   vinegar
2 teaspoons dry mustard powder
1 teaspoon Worcestershire sauce
Pinch ground cinnamon
1-1/4 cups tomato juice
2 large onions, chopped
1 pound smoked ham, cubed
Chopped fresh chives to garnish

In a large saucepan, cover beans with cold water and soak overnight. Rinse beans and add enough water to cover beans by 1 inch. Bring to a boil and boil rapidly 15 minutes. Cover and simmer 1 hour, until beans are tender. Preheat oven to 275F (135C). Drain beans into a large casserole dish and reserve cooking liquid. In a medium-size bowl, combine brown sugar, salt, molasses, vinegar, dry mustard, Worcestershire sauce, cinnamon and tomato juice and stir into beans. Add onions and enough of reserved cooking liquid to just cover beans. Cover casserole and bake in preheated oven 2 hours, checking occasionally to add more cooking liquid, if necessary. Remove lid and stir in cubed ham. Return to oven 1 hour. To serve, garnish with chopped chives.

Makes 6 to 8 servings.

Note: Serve with plenty of crusty bread and butter.

Stuffed Eggs

8 large eggs, hard-cooked
1/2 (6-1/2-oz.) can tuna, drained
2 tablespoons mayonnaise
2 teaspoons lemon juice
1 teaspoon chopped fresh parsley
1 teaspoon tomato paste
1 teaspoon Worcestershire sauce
Salt and pepper to taste
2 ounces cooked peeled shrimp, finely
    diced
Lettuce leaves
Triangles of lemon, black lumpfish roe,
    whole cooked peeled shrimp and
    sprigs of dill to garnish

Peel eggs and cut in half lengthwise. Remove yolks and divide equally between 2 medium-size bowls. In 1 bowl, add tuna, 1/2 of mayonnaise, 1/2 of lemon juice and parsley. Mash to form a rough chunky paste. In remaining bowl, add remaining mayonnaise, remaining lemon juice, tomato paste and Worcestershire sauce and mix well. Season with salt and pepper. Stir in diced shrimp. Pile spoonfuls of stuffing into eggs. Arrange eggs on lettuce leaves. Garnish tuna-stuffed eggs with triangles of lemon and spoonfuls of lumpfish roe. Garnish shrimp-stuffed eggs with whole shrimp and sprigs of dill.

Makes 4 servings.

Pear & Loganberry Soup

2 cooking pears, peeled, cored
Grated peel and juice of 1/2 lemon
1/3 cup sugar
2 cups white wine
1 cup plus 2 tablespoons water
2 teaspoons cornstarch
12 ounces loganberries
Toasted sliced almonds

Slice pears thinly and place in a large saucepan. Add lemon juice, sugar, 1 cup of wine and 1 cup of water. Bring to a boil, stirring continuously. In a small bowl, mix cornstarch with remaining water, then mix in lemon peel and pour into soup. Cook until thick and glossy. Remove from heat and cool. Sieve 1/2 of loganberies. Stir loganberry puree and remaining loganberries into soup. Chill. To serve, pour in remaining wine and sprinkle with sliced almonds.

Makes 4 servings.

Note: Serve with scoops of vanilla ice cream for a really special treat.

Crunchy Potato Skins

6 medium-size baking potatoes
6 slices bacon
2 small avocados
1 garlic clove, crushed
2 or 3 teaspoons lemon juice
2 or 3 teaspoons plain yogurt
2 drops hot-pepper sauce
Salt and pepper to taste
1/4 cup vegetable oil
Sprigs of watercress to garnish

Preheat oven to 400F (205C). Scrub potatoes and prick all over with a fork. Bake in preheated oven 1 hour, until just tender. Remove potatoes from oven and increase heat to 425F (220C). In a medium-size skillet, cook bacon until crisp and golden. Drain on paper towels. Peel avocados and remove pits. In a medium-size bowl, mash avocados. Stir in garlic, lemon juice, yogurt and hot-pepper sauce. Season with salt and pepper. Pour oil into a shallow roasting dish and heat in oven. Cut potatoes in half lengthwise and scoop out most of pulp, leaving a layer next to skin. Reserve pulp for another use. Sprinkle skins with salt and place in hot oil, hollow-side down. Baste with hot oil and turn hollow side up. Bake in oven 25 minutes, basting frequently, until potatoes are golden and crunchy. Drain potatoes on paper towels. Fill cavities with avocado cream. Cut bacon in small strips and arrange over avocado cream. Serve at once, garnished with sprigs of watercress.

Makes 4 servings.

Bacon & Tuna Samosa Rolls

6 bacon slices
6 green onions, sliced
1 to 2 teaspoons garam masala
8 ounces potatoes, cooked, diced
1 (3-1/2-oz.) can tuna
1 tablespoon chopped fresh parsley
Salt and pepper to taste
4 sheets filo pastry, thawed if frozen
1 egg white, lightly whisked
Vegetable oil for frying
Sprigs of cilantro to garnish

In a medium-size skillet, cook bacon until crisp and golden. Drain on paper towels and cut in small pieces. Add green onions and garam masala to skillet and sauté 1 minute. Stir in bacon, potatoes, tuna and parsley. Season with salt and pepper and cool. Cut each pastry sheet crosswise in 4 (4-inch) strips. Place a spoonful of potato filling at top of each strip. Roll up to halfway along strip, then flatten 2 edges and fold in to enclose filling completely. Resume rolling and seal end with a small amount of egg white. Repeat with remaining rolls. Heat oil in a deep-fryer to 375F (190C). Carefully fry batches of 3 or 4 rolls 2 to 3 minutes, turning frequently, until golden and crisp. Drain on paper towels. Garnish with sprigs of cilantro and serve warm.

Makes 16 rolls.

Morning Croustades

1 stale large white loaf of bread
10 tablespoons butter, melted
4 bacon slices
4 cherry tomatoes
4 cocktail sausages
1 tablespoon vegetable oil
6 button mushrooms, halved
4 quail eggs
Sprigs of parsley to garnish

Preheat oven to 375F (190C). Cut crusts off bread to make a 10" x 3" x 3" rectangle. Cut in 4 equal slices to make 4 (3"x 3" x 2-1/2") squares. Score a 2" x 2" square in center of each bread cube, leaving a 1/2-inch border of bread. Work a knife around central square, cutting down to within 1/2 inch of bottom. Remove inner square of bread; reserve for another use. Brush bread cubes with melted butter and place on a baking sheet. Bake in preheated oven 15 minutes, until crisp and golden. Roll up bacon slices and secure with wooden picks. Preheat broiler. Thread tomatoes on wooden picks with bacon and broil under preheated grill 4 to 5 minutes, until cooked. In a small skillet, fry sausages in oil until brown. Add mushrooms and cook 2 to 3 minutes. In a small saucepan, plunge eggs into boiling water 2 minutes, then drain. Refresh in cold water and peel. Arrange bacon rolls, tomatoes, sausages, mushrooms and eggs in bread cubes. Garnish with sprigs of parsley and serve at once.

Makes 4 servings.

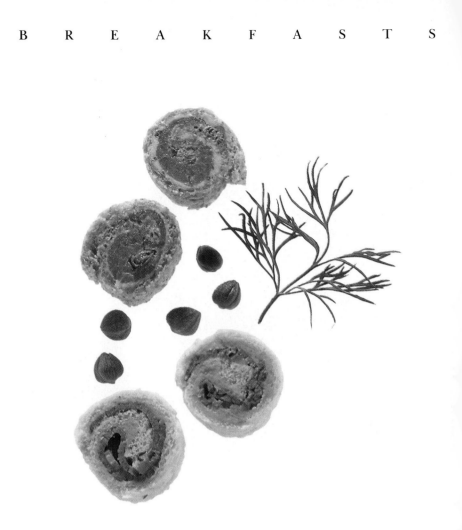

Pinwheels

5 very thin slices fresh white bread
5 very thin slices fresh whole-wheat
   bread
8 tablespoons butter, softened
1 to 2 teaspoons prepared mustard
3 ounces thinly sliced pastrami
2 teaspoons finely chopped gherkin
   pickles
2 teaspoons chopped fresh dill
3 ounces thinly sliced smoked salmon
Freshly ground pepper
2 teaspoons finely chopped capers
Mustard and sprigs of cress to garnish

Cut crusts off bread. Divide butter equally between 2 small bowls. Beat mustard into 1 bowl of butter and spread over white bread. Lay pastrami over bread, leaving 1-1/2 inches of butter uncovered. Sprinkle with pickles. Beat dill into remaining butter and spread over whole-wheat bread. Lay salmon over butter, leaving 1-1/2 inches of bread uncovered. Sprinkle with pepper and capers. Roll up bread tightly, jelly-roll style, ending with buttered edge. Wrap each roll tightly in foil and chill at least 1 hour. Unwrap and cut each roll crosswise in 5 to 6 slices. Serve pinwheels garnished with mustard and cress.

Makes 25 to 30 pinwheels.

Shrimp Toasts

6 ounces cooked peeled shrimp
1 (1/2-inch) piece gingerroot, peeled,
  crushed
1 garlic clove, crushed
2 green onions, finely chopped
2 teaspoons light soy sauce
1 teaspoon plum sauce
1 tablespoon cornstarch
1 small egg, beaten
1 tablespoon plus 1 teaspoon sesame
  seeds
4 thin slices white bread, crusts removed
Vegetable oil
Cucumber and green onion strips to
  garnish

In a blender or food processor fitted with the metal blade, process shrimp, gingerroot, garlic and green onions 30 seconds. In a medium-size bowl, mix soy sauce, plum sauce, cornstarch and egg; stir in shrimp mixture and sesame seeds and mix well. Spread shrimp mixture over bread, pressing down firmly. In a large skillet, heat 3/4 inch of oil. Fry bread, shrimp-sides down, 2 to 3 minutes, until golden, pressing down well in oil. Turn over and fry 1 minute. Drain on paper towels. Cut in fingers and serve at once, garnished with cucumber and green onion strips.

Makes 4 servings.

Tropical Salad

2 large mangoes
2 papayas
2 large avocados
Grated peel and juice of 1/2 lime
2 ounces watercress
3 sprigs parsley
2 teaspoons tarragon leaves
2/3 cup mayonnaise
1 tablespoon plus 1 teaspoon dairy sour
  cream
1/2 to 1 teaspoon superfine sugar
Sprigs of herbs and 1 teaspoon pickled
  green peppercorns to garnish

Peel mangoes. Remove pits and slice crosswise in strips. Halve papayas and remove black seeds. Peel and slice in strips. Halve avocados and remove pits. Peel and slice in strips. Sprinkle fruit with 1/2 of lime juice and arrange on a serving dish. In a small saucepan, blanch watercress, parsley and tarragon in boiling water 45 seconds, until soft but bright green. Refresh under cold running water, drain and pat dry with paper towels. In a blender or food processor fitted with the metal blade, process blanched herbs and mayonnaise 1 minute, until smooth and green. Stir in remaining lime juice, sour cream, lime peel and sugar to taste. Spoon herbed mayonnaise over prepared fruits and garnish with sprigs of herbs and green peppercorns.

Makes 4 servings.

Crepe Cups

1 cup all-purpose flour
1/4 teaspoon salt
1 tablespoon plus 2 teaspoons chopped
   fresh parsley
1 large egg, beaten
2/3 cup milk
2/3 cup beer
Vegetable oil for frying
1 pound cooked boneless skinned
   chicken
1/4 cup mayonnaise
1/4 cup dairy sour cream
2 teaspoons chopped fresh tarragon
2 teaspoons lemon juice
1 teaspoon grated lemon peel
Salt and pepper to taste
1/3 cup pumpkin seeds
1/4 cup pine nuts
Lemon triangles to garnish

Sift flour and salt into a large bowl. Add 1 tablespoon of parsley, egg, milk and beer and beat well to make a smooth batter. Heat a griddle and brush with oil. Pour in enough batter to make a 5-inch crepe and cook 1 minute, until golden. Turn over and cook other side. Repeat with remaining batter to prepare 11 more crepes. Preheat oven to 375F (190C). Generously grease a 12-cup muffin pan and line with crepes. Bake in preheated oven 10 to 15 minutes, until crisp. Dice chicken in 1/4-inch chunks. In a medium-size bowl, combine chicken chunks, mayonnaise, sour cream, tarragon and lemon juice and peel. Season with salt and pepper. Stir in pumpkin seeds. Spoon mixture into crepe cups and sprinkle with pine nuts and remaining parsley. Serve garnished with lemon triangles.

Makes 12 cups.

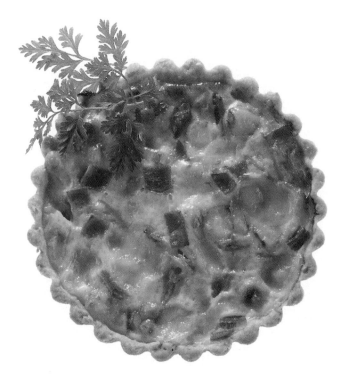

Swiss Tartlets

3/4 cup all-purpose flour
1 tablespoon regular rolled oats
1 teaspoon dry mustard powder
5-1/2 tablespoons butter
About 2 tablespoons water
4 ounces smoked ham, diced
4 ounces Emmenthaler cheese, diced
1 egg, beaten
2/3 cup half and half
Salt and pepper to taste
Grated nutmeg
Sprigs of chervil to garnish

In a blender or food processor fitted with the metal blade, process flour, oats, dry mustard and butter 45 seconds. Add water and process 15 seconds or until pastry binds together. Divide in 4 equal pieces. Roll out pastry on a floured surface. Line 4 (4-1/2-inch) flan pans with pastry. Chill 10 minutes. Preheat oven to 400F (205C). Divide ham and cheese equally among pastry shells. In a small bowl, mix egg and half and half. Season with salt and pepper. Pour over ham and cheese and sprinkle with grated nutmeg. Bake in preheated oven 25 minutes, until golden and set. Serve warm, garnished with sprigs of chervil.

Makes 4 servings.

Sausage Covered Eggs

1 pound pork sausage
Salt and pepper to taste
12 quail eggs, hard-cooked, peeled
1/2 cup all-purpose flour, sifted
1 egg, lightly beaten
1/2 cup fresh whole-wheat bread crumbs
Vegetable oil for deep-frying
1/2 cup mayonnaise
1/4 cup dairy sour cream
2 teaspoons Dijon-style mustard
2 teaspoon chopped fresh parsley

Place sausage in a blender or food processor fitted with the metal blade. Season with salt and pepper and process until smooth. Divide sausage in 12 equal portions. Flatten in rounds and place 1 egg in center of each round. Wrap sausage around eggs to enclose completely. Roll each roll first in flour, then in beaten egg and then in bread crumbs. Chill 15 minutes. In a large saucepan, heat oil until very hot. Deep-fry rolls 3 minutes, until golden. Drain on paper towels. In a small bowl, blend mayonnaise, sour cream, mustard and parsley. Serve rolls warm with herbed mayonnaise.

Makes 4 servings.

Atholl Brose

1/2 cup regular rolled oats
1 tablespoon honey
1 tablespoon whiskey, if desired
1-1/4 cups plain yogurt
2/3 cup whipping cream
1 cup raspberries

In a large skillet, heat oats until toasted and golden-brown, stirring constantly. Cool. In a large bowl, combine honey, whiskey, yogurt and whipping cream and whisk until stiff. Fold in most of toasted oats and 3/4 cup of raspberries. Spoon creamy mixture into dessert dishes. Sprinkle each with remaining toasted oats and garnish with remaining raspberries.

Makes 4 servings.

Lemon Geranium Syllabub

Pared peel and juice of 1 lemon
12 large scented lemon geranium leaves
1-3/4 cups whipping cream
1/3 cup superfine sugar
1/2 cup dry white wine
2 ounces ratafia cookies (macaroons)
Small geranium leaves and lemon slices
    to decorate

In a small saucepan, place strips of lemon peel and large geranium leaves. Pour in 2/3 cup of whipping cream. Bring to a boil very slowly, stirring constantly. Remove from heat and cool completely, stirring occasionally. In a large bowl, combine lemon juice, sugar and wine; stir until sugar completely dissolves. Strain cooked cream-mixture and pour into wine mixture, stirring constantly. Using an electric mixer, whip until syllabub stands in soft peaks, about 10 to 15 minutes. Divide cookies among 6 dessert dishes and spoon syllabub on top. Decorate with small geranium leaves and lemon slices.

Makes 6 servings.

——— Gooseberry-Rhubarb Fool ———

4 ounces rhubarb, chopped
1/3 cup superfine sugar
1/4 cup water
3/4 cup gooseberries, ends removed
3/4 cup fromage frais or ricotta cheese
1-1/4 cups whipping cream
Red and green food coloring, if desired
Ladyfinger cookies to serve

In a medium-size saucepan, combine rhubarb, 1/2 of sugar and 1/2 of water. In another medium-size saucepan, combine gooseberries and remaining sugar and water. Bring both to a boil and simmer uncovered 15 to 20 minutes, until fruit is soft and pulpy. Remove from heat and cool completely. In a medium-size bowl, drain syrup from both rhubarb and gooseberries and mix. Stir 1/2 of fromage frais or ricotta cheese into rhubarb and remainder into gooseberries. In a medium-size bowl, whip cream until stiff and fold half into each fruit mixture. Add food coloring, if desired. Spoon alternate layers of rhubarb, gooseberry and teaspoons of rhubarb-gooseberry syrup into glasses, finishing with a spoonful of syrup. Chill and serve with cookies.

Makes 4 to 6 servings.

Berry Compote

1 cup loganberries
1 cup raspberries
1 cup black currants
1 cup strawberries, halved
1/3 cup sugar
1 tablespoon lemon juice
1 tablespoon water
1/2 vanilla bean
Cookies to serve, if desired

In a large saucepan, combine fruit, sugar, lemon juice, water and vanilla bean. Gently stir over very low heat until sugar dissolves. Remove from heat and cool. Discard vanilla bean. Pour fruit into a glass serving bowl and chill. Serve with cookies, if desired.

Makes 4 servings.

Mushroom Bundles

4 sheets filo pastry, thawed if frozen
3 tablespoons butter, melted
8 ounces button mushrooms
2-3/4 ounces Boursin cheese
Chives to garnish

Preheat oven to 425F (220C). Brush 2 sheets of filo with some of butter and lay remaining 2 sheets of pastry on top. Cut each double sheet in about 12 (3-inch) squares. Remove stalks from mushrooms and fill each cavity with 1/4 teaspoonful of cheese. Place each mushroom cheese-side up in center of a square of pastry. Bring up edges to completely enclose mushrooms, leaving pastry edges pointing upwards. Brush tops of pastry with remaining butter. Bake in preheated oven 5 minutes, until crisp and golden. Cool slightly. Tie a chive around top of each bundle and serve warm.

Makes 24 bundles.

—— Chicken & Asparagus Terrine ——

8 ounces asparagus
1 pound cooked skinned boneless
  chicken breasts, coarsely chopped
1 tablespoon chopped fresh tarragon
Grated peel and juice of 1/2 lemon
2 eggs, separated
3/4 cup dairy sour cream
Salt and pepper to taste
2/3 cup mayonnaise

Preheat oven to 325F (165C). Lightly grease a 9" x 5" loaf pan. Cut asparagus into 1-inch lengths. In a medium-size saucepan, drop asparagus into boiling salted water and cook 2 minutes. Drain and refresh under cold running water. In a blender or food processor fitted with the metal blade, process chicken, tarragon and lemon peel 30 to 45 seconds. Stir in egg yolks and 1/4 cup of sour cream. Season with salt and pepper. In a small bowl, whisk egg whites until stiff, then fold into chicken mixture. Fold in asparagus and pour into greased loaf pan. Cover and place in a roasting pan half filled with water. Bake in preheated oven 1 hour. Cool. In a small bowl, mix lemon juice, remaining sour cream and mayonnaise and serve with slices of terrine.

Makes 6 to 8 servings.

Mushroom Roll

1/4 cup herb butter, see Note
12 ounces mixed mushrooms, finely
  chopped
1 tablespoon plus 1 teaspoon all-purpose
  flour
4 large eggs, separated
3 tablespoons chopped fresh parsley
5 ounces Boursin cheese
3/4 cup cottage cheese
2 teaspoons chopped fresh chives
1 tablespoon plus 1 teaspoon grated
  Parmesan cheese
Sprigs of parsley to garnish

Preheat oven to 400F (205C). Grease a
jelly-roll pan and line with parchment
paper. Melt butter in a large skillet.
Gently cook mushrooms 5 to 7 minutes,
until softened. Add flour and bring to a
boil, stirring constantly until thick. Remove from heat and cool slightly. In a
medium-size bowl, whisk egg whites
until stiff. Beat egg yolks into mushroom mixture, then fold in beaten egg
whites and 2 tablespoons of chopped
parsley. Pour into prepared pan and
bake in preheated oven 12 to 15 minutes. Cool. In a small bowl, beat Boursin cheese, cottage cheese and chives.

Sprinkle a sheet of parchment paper
with remaining parsley and Parmesan
cheese. Turn savory cake out onto
parchment paper and spread with
cheese mixture. Roll up, jelly-roll style,
and place on a long serving dish. Serve
in thick slices, garnished with sprigs of
parsley.

Makes 4 to 6 servings.

Note: To prepare herb butter, mix
1-1/2 teaspoons finely chopped fresh
herbs and 1/4 cup softened butter.

Cheesy Ham Croissants

4 thin slices smoked ham
1 teaspoon prepared mild mustard
1 teaspoon chopped chives
4 thin slices Gouda cheese
4 croissants

Preheat oven to 400F (205C). Spread ham slices with mustard and sprinkle chives over cheese slices. Cut each slice of ham and cheese in half. Place 1 slice of cheese on top of 1 slice of ham, top with second ham slice and finish with cheese. Repeat to prepare 4 ham and cheese stacks. Split croissants in half and place a ham and cheese stack into each. Wrap croissants in foil and bake in preheated oven 10 minutes. Open foil and bake 2 minutes more, until croissants are crisp. Serve at once.

Makes 4 servings.

Note: Serve with a crisp green salad.

Bacon & Herb Scones

4 bacon slices
2 cups self-rising flour
1 teaspoon baking powder
1 teaspoon dry mustard powder
4 tablespoons butter, chilled
2 tablespoons chopped fresh parsley
1 tablespoon chopped fresh chives
2/3 cup milk

Preheat oven to 425F (220C). In a medium-size skillet, cook bacon until crisp and golden. Drain on paper towels. Cool and chop finely. Sift flour, baking powder and dry mustard into a large bowl. Cut in butter. Stir in bacon, parsley and chives and enough milk to make a soft light dough. Turn onto a floured surface and knead lightly. Roll or pat out to about 3/4 inch thick and cut in rounds using a 2-inch cutter. Place rounds on a baking sheet and brush tops with milk. Bake in preheated oven 10 to 15 minutes, until well risen and golden.

Makes 8 servings.

Cucumber-Shrimp Mousse

1 (8-oz.) package cream cheese, softened
1 tablespoon plus 1 teaspoon fromage
   frais or ricotta cheese
1 tablespoon butter
6 green onions, finely sliced
1 (1/4-oz.) envelope unflavored gelatin
   (about 1 tablespoon)
Juice of 1/2 lemon
1 medium-size cucumber, finely diced
   (about 1 cup)
Salt and pepper to taste
3/4 cup mayonnaise
1 teaspoon tomato paste
1/2 teaspoon Worcestershire sauce
1 teaspoon lemon juice
6 ounces cooked peeled shrimp
Whole cooked peeled shrimp and lemon
   slices to garnish

Oil 6 (3-inch) rum baba molds. In a medium-size bowl, beat cream cheese and fromage frais or ricotta cheese until smooth. Set aside. In a medium-size skillet, melt butter. Gently sauté green onions in butter until softened; drain on paper towels. In a small bowl, sprinkle gelatin over lemon juce and let stand 2 to 3 minutes, until softened. Set bowl of gelatin in a saucepan of hot water and stir until dissolved and quite hot. Cool. Combine cheese mixture, green onions and cucumber. Season with salt and pepper. Pour in gelatin and mix well. Spoon into oiled molds and chill 2 to 4 hours, until set. In a small bowl, combine mayonnaise, tomato paste, Worcestershire sauce and lemon juice and stir in shrimp. Turn out cucumber mousses onto individual plates and spoon shrimp mixture into center of each. Garnish with whole shrimp and lemon slices.

Makes 6 servings.

Sesame Breakfast Fingers

2/3 (17-1/4-oz.) package frozen puff
  pastry, thawed
6 bacon slices
1 tablespoon plus 1 teaspoon Dijon-style
  mustard
1 egg, beaten
3/4 cup shredded Cheddar cheese (3 oz.)
1 tablespoon plus 1 teaspoon sesame
  seeds

Preheat oven to 425F (220C). Roll out
pastry to a 20" x 12" rectangle and cut
in half. In a medium-size skillet, cook
bacon until crisp and golden and cut in
strips. Spread 1/2 of pastry with mustard and sprinkle with bacon strips.
Brush remaining half of pastry with
beaten egg and lay egg-side down on
top of bacon; press down well. Brush
with beaten egg and sprinkle with
cheese, then with sesame seeds. Cut in
3" x 2" fingers and place on baking
sheets. Bake in preheated oven 10 to 15
minutes, until cheese is golden and pastry cooked.

Makes 40 fingers.

Seafood Filled Brioche

2 tablespoons butter
6 green onions, chopped
Pinch saffron strands
2/3 cup whipping cream
1 tablespoon plus 1 teaspoon sherry
4 ounces cooked shrimp, peeled
24 cooked mussels
Salt and pepper to taste
2 teaspoons lemon juice
1 tablespoon chopped fresh parsley
6 prepared Brioche, page 30

Preheat oven to 350F (175C). Melt butter in a medium-size skillet. Add green onions and sauté 1 minute. Add saffron, whipping cream and sherry and boil until reduced and thickened. Stir in shrimp and mussels and heat through. Remove from heat, season with salt and pepper and stir in lemon juice. Stir in chopped parsley. Remove tops from brioche and scoop out and discard insides. Spoon in seafood filling and replace tops. Place in an ovenproof dish, cover with foil and bake in preheated oven 10 minutes, until hot.

Makes 6 servings.

Gazpacho

3 garlic cloves
1 pound tomatoes, peeled
1 cucumber, chopped
1/2 red bell pepper, chopped
6 green onions, chopped
1-1/2 cups tomato juice
1 tablespoon red wine vinegar
1 teaspoon sugar
1/2 teaspoon salt
1 tablespoon olive oil
4 thick slices bread
2 tablespoons vegetable oil

Crush 1 garlic clove. In a blender or food processor fitted with the metal blade, process crushed garlic, tomatoes, cucumber, bell pepper, green onions, tomato juice, vinegar, sugar, salt and olive oil until smooth. Pour into a large bowl and chill. Remove crusts from bread and cut slices in 1/2-inch cubes. In a medium-size skillet, heat vegetable oil and remaining garlic. Remove garlic and fry bread cubes until crisp and golden. Drain on paper towels. Serve gazpacho in chilled bowls; pass croutons separately.

Makes 6 to 8 servings.

Lemon Shrimp

3 (4-1/4-oz.) cans shrimp
Grated peel and juice of 1/2 lemon
16 tablespoons butter
1 tablespoon chopped fresh parsley
Large pinch ground mace
Freshly ground pepper
Lemon balm leaves

Drain shrimp and place in a bowl. Sprinkle with lemon juice and chill 10 minutes. In a small saucepan, melt 10-1/2 tablespoons of butter. Add drained shrimp to melted butter. Stir in lemon peel, parsley, mace and pepper and cook over low heat 2 minutes. Spoon mixture into 4 small ramekin dishes and chill until set. In a small saucepan, melt remaining butter and strain through a piece of muslin to remove white sediment. Top each ramekin with a lemon balm leaf and spoon clarified butter over top.

Makes 4 servings.

Note: Serve with triangles of hot toast and lemon wedges.

Salmon Puffs

Salmon Mousse:
4 ounces cooked salmon
1 tablespoon plus 1 teaspoon mayonnaise
Grated peel and juice of 1 lemon
Salt and pepper to taste
1 (1/4-oz.) envelope unflavored gelatin
  (about 1 tablespoon)
1-1/4 cups whipping cream, lightly
  whipped

Dill Sauce:
1-1/4 cups mayonnaise
Juice of 1/2 lemon
2 tablespoons chopped fresh dill
Salt and pepper to taste

Choux Paste:
2/3 cup water
4 tablespoons butter
3/4 cup all-purpose flour, sifted
2 eggs, beaten

Sprigs of dill to garnish

To prepare mousse, in a blender or food processor, process salmon, mayonnaise and lemon peel until smooth. Season with salt and pepper. In a small bowl, sprinkle gelatin over lemon juice and let stand 2 to 3 minutes, until soft-ened. Set gelatin in hot water and stir until dissolved and hot. Cool. Fold whipped cream into salmon mixture and stir in gelatin. Chill 2 to 3 hours, until set. To prepare dill sauce, in a small bowl, beat mayonnaise, lemon juice and dill. Season with salt and pepper. Preheat oven to 400F (205C). To prepare choux paste, heat water and butter in a medium-size saucepan until just boiling. Add flour and beat until smooth. Remove from heat and beat in eggs, a small amount at a time, until mixture is smooth and glossy. Using a pastry bag fitted with a plain nozzle, pipe mixture in 18 small balls onto a wetted nonstick baking sheet. Bake in a preheated oven 15 to 20 minutes, until golden and puffy. Cool. Make a small hole in bottom of each puff. Using a pastry bag fitted with a plain nozzle, pipe salmon mousse into puffs. Pile puffs onto a plate and pour dill sauce over puffs. Serve at once, garnished with dill.

Makes 6 servings.

Danish Windmill Pastries

2 cups bread flour
2 tablespoons lard
Pinch of salt
1 tablespoon plus 2 teaspoons sugar
2/3 (1/4-oz.) envelope fast-rising yeast
   (2 teaspoons)
1 egg, beaten
1/4 cup water
8 tablespoons butter, softened
10 apricot halves
Beaten egg to glaze
3 tablespoons powdered sugar
1 tablespoon lemon juice

Oil a plastic bag. Sift flour into a large bowl and cut in lard. Stir in salt, sugar, yeast and egg. In a small saucepan, heat water to 125F (50C) to 130F (55C). Mix into flour mixture to form a soft dough.

Knead until smooth, then place in oiled plastic bag. Chill 10 minutes. Place butter between 2 pieces of plastic wrap and flatten to a 5-inch square. Roll out dough on a floured surface to a 12" x 10" rectangle. Place butter in center. Bring 2 sides of dough over to overlap each other and enclose butter, then bring top and bottom ends over. Turn over and gently roll to a rectangle about 3 times as long as width. Fold into thirds and repeat rolling and folding 3 more times. Return to oiled plastic bag and chill at least 1 hour. Roll out dough to a 20" x 8" rectangle and cut in 4-inch squares. Make a cut at each corner diagonally towards middle and fold 1 point from each corner into middle like a windmill. Top with an apricot half and brush with beaten egg. Cover and let stand in a warm place 20 minutes, until risen. Meanwhile, preheat oven to 425F (220C). Bake in preheated oven 10 minutes, until golden. Cool on a wire rack. In a small bowl, mix powdered sugar and lemon juice and brush over warm pastries.

Makes 10 pastries.

Caribbean Stack

2 ounces creamed coconut, grated
2/3 cup warm water
3/4 cup all-purpose flour
1/3 cup shredded unsweetened coconut
2 eggs, beaten
1-1/4 cups pineapple juice
Vegetable oil for frying
1/2 small pineapple, peeled, cored, finely
   chopped
1 tablespoon cornstarch
Juice of 1 orange
1 tablespoon plus 1 teaspoon dark rum
2 bananas, thinly sliced
2 kiwifruit, finely chopped
2 passion fruit, halved, seeded, pulp
   removed
Toasted coconut and whipped cream, if
   desired, to serve

Place creamed coconut in a small bowl. Pour in warm water and allow coconut to soften. In a blender or food processor fitted with the metal blade, process creamed coconut liquid, flour, shredded coconut, eggs and 2/3 cup pineapple juice until smooth. Heat a griddle and brush with oil. Prepare 8 thin pancakes and keep warm between 2 plates set over a pan of simmering water. In a small saucepan, combine remaining pineapple juice and pineapple and bring slowly to a boil. In a small bowl, blend cornstarch, orange juice and rum and stir into pineapple mixture. Cook until thickened and glossy. Remove from heat and stir in bananas, kiwifruit and passion fruit pulp and cool slightly. Spread 1 pancake with fruit mixture and top with a second pancake. Repeat using all pancakes and filling, finishing with a pancake. Sprinkle with toasted coconut and serve cut in wedges with whipped cream, if desired.

Makes 6 to 8 servings.

Savarin

1 cup bread flour
1/4 teaspoon salt
2/3 (1/4-oz.) envelope fast-rising yeast
(2 teaspoons)
1/4 cup milk
4 tablespoons butter
2 large eggs, beaten
1/3 cup sugar
3/4 cup water
Pared peel 1 lemon
3 tablespoons apricot jam, sieved
Fresh fruit and whipped cream, if
desired, to serve

Grease and flour a 7-inch ring mold. Sift flour and salt into a large bowl. Stir in yeast. In a small saucepan, heat milk and butter to 125F (50C) to 130F (55C). Stir milk mixture into dry ingredients, then stir in eggs and beat well, at least 3 minutes. Pour into greased mold. Cover and let stand in a warm place until risen over top of mold. Meanwhile, preheat oven to 400F (205C). Bake in preheated oven 20 minutes. Cool slightly in mold, then turn out onto a wire rack. Prick savarin well with a small skewer. In a small saucepan, dissolve sugar in water. Add lemon peel and bring to a boil. Simmer 5 minutes, remove from heat and cool. While savarin is still warm, spoon syrup over top, reserving 1 tablespoon of syrup. In a small saucepan, warm jam and reserved syrup and brush over savarin. Place savarin on a serving plate. Fill center with fresh fruit and serve with whipped cream, if desired.

Makes 6 servings.

Peach Cream Brûlée

2 egg yolks
1 tablespoon sugar
Few drops vanilla extract
1-1/4 cups whipping cream
3 ripe peaches
1-1/4 cups packed light-brown sugar

In a medium-size bowl, beat egg yolks, sugar and vanilla until pale and fluffy. In a small saucepan, heat whipping cream until just boiling and whisk into egg mixture. Return mixture to pan and cook over low heat, stirring constantly, until thickened; do not boil. Remove from the heat and cool slightly. Peel, halve and remove pits from peaches. Place half a peach in bottom of each of 6 ramekin dishes. Pour cooled custard over peaches and chill 6 to 12 hours, until firm. Preheat broiler. Sprinkle custards with a thick layer of brown sugar and broil until brown sugar dissolves and bubbles. Cool before serving.

Makes 6 servings.

Champagne & Mint Granita

3/4 cup superfine sugar
Pared peel and juice of 1 lemon
2 large bunches mint
1-3/4 cups water
1-3/4 cups champagne-type sparkling wine
Lemon slices and sprigs of mint to garnish

In a medium-size saucepan, combine sugar, lemon peel and juice, 1 bunch of mint and water. Heat gently, stirring constantly, until sugar dissolves. Bring to a boil and boil rapidly 5 minutes. Strain into a large bowl and add remaining mint. Cool. Remove mint and stir champagne into syrup. Pour into a shallow freezer container and freeze until slushy. Remove from freezer and beat or whisk until smooth. Repeat this process again, then freeze until set. Place granita in refrigerator 20 minutes before serving to make it easier to scoop. Spoon granita into frosted champagne glasses and garnish with lemon slices and sprigs of mint.

Makes 6 servings.

Tropical Cocktail

2 ounces creamed coconut, grated
1-3/4 cups pineapple juice
1 large banana
1/3 cup white rum
1/3 cup half and half
1-1/4 cups milk
Ice cubes
Wedges of pineapple to decorate

Place creamed coconut and pineapple juice in a blender or food processor fitted with the metal blade; let stand 10 minutes. Add remaining ingredients and process until smooth. Pour into glasses, add ice cubes and decorate with wedges of pineapple.

Makes 4 servings.

Strawberry Foam

1-1/4 cups strawberries, hulled
1/4 cup superfine sugar
Pared peel of 1/2 lemon
2 teaspoons lemon juice
2 tablespoons Cointreau
2 (750-ml.) bottles chilled champagne
Frozen strawberries and borage flowers
    to decorate

In a blender or food processor fitted with the metal blade, process 1-1/4 cups strawberries to a puree. Pour puree into a small saucepan and add sugar and lemon peel and juice. Slowly bring to a boil, stirring constantly. Remove from heat and cool. Strain and stir in Cointreau. Pour a small amount of strawbery syrup into tall glasses and fill with chilled champagne. Decorate each glass with a frozen strawberry and borage flowers. Serve at once.

Makes 4 to 6 servings.

Hot Chocolate

5 ounces semisweet chocolate
2 tablespoons hot water
3 cups milk
Few drops vanilla extract
4 marshmallows
2/3 cup whipping cream
2 to 3 teaspoons grated orange peel
1 teaspoon finely grated semisweet
  chocolate

In a medium-size saucepan, melt chocolate in hot water. Add milk and bring to a boil, stirring constantly. Remove from heat, add vanilla and whisk. Put a marshmallow into each of 4 heat-proof glasses and pour in hot chocolate. In a small bowl, whisk whipping cream and orange peel until it forms soft peaks. Spoon onto hot chocolate and sprinkle with grated chocolate.

Makes 4 to 6 servings.

Spiced Orange Tea

1 large orange
4 whole cloves
1 (2-inch) cinnamon stick
1 cup fresh orange juice
2 cups prepared lapsang soochong tea
1 to 2 tablespoons honey
1/2 cup pineapple juice
1/2 teaspoon freshly grated nutmeg
Slices of orange and ground nutmeg to
    decorate

Stud orange with cloves. Prick orange all over and place in a large saucepan. Add cinnamon stick and orange juice. Bring to a boil, then simmer 5 minutes. Remove from heat and let stand 30 minutes to infuse. Remove orange and spices and add tea and honey to taste. Stir in pineapple juice and 1/2 teaspoon nutmeg and reheat gently. Pour into heatproof glasses and decorate with slices of orange and a sprinkling of nutmeg.

Makes 4 servings.

Peach Cooler

2 large peaches, peeled, pitted
Juice of 1/2 lemon
2 (6-oz.) cartons peach yogurt
2 cups milk
Ice cubes
Slices of peaches to decorate

In a blender or food processor fitted
with the metal blade, process peeled
peaches, lemon juice, yogurt and milk
until smooth. Fill glasses with ice cubes
and pour in peach cooler. Decorate
with slices of peaches.

Makes 4 to 6 servings.

Rose Petal Infusion

3 rosehip teabags
1-1/4 cups boiling water
2 to 3 tablespoons rosehip syrup
Handful scented rose petals
3 tablespoons triple-strength rose water
2-1/2 cups carbonated water
Ice cubes
Additional rose petals to decorate

Place teabags in a medium-size bowl and cover with boiling water. Let stand 10 minutes to infuse, then remove teabags and cool. When completly cold, stir in rosehip syrup, rose petals and rose water and let stand 30 minutes to infuse. Strain and stir in carbonated water. Fill glasses with ice cubes and pour in rose petal infusion. Decorate with additional rose petals.

Makes 4 to 6 servings.

Note: Triple-strength rose water may be obtained from specialty food stores.

— Raspberry Cooler —

Pared peel and juice of 1/2 lemon
1-1/4 cups frozen raspberries
5 cups sparkling white wine
1/4 cup Benedictine
2-1/4 cups carbonated lemon-flavored
   mineral water
Ice cubes

Cut lemon peel in julienne strips and
place in a large punch bowl. Add lemon
juice and raspberries. Pour in wine and
Benedictine. Stir well and let stand 5
minutes to infuse. Add carbonated
water and ice cubes and serve at once in
glasses.

Makes 8 servings.

Mulled Wine

1 lemon
4 whole cloves
1 (750-ml.) bottle red wine
1 (2-inch) cinnamon stick
2 blades mace
Pared peel and juice of 2 oranges
1/2 teaspoon freshly ground nutmeg
1/3 cup sugar
1/2 cup brandy
Slices of kumquats and freshly ground
    nutmeg to serve

Stud lemon with cloves. In a large saucepan, combine lemon, wine, cinnamon stick, mace, orange peel and juice, 1/2 teaspoon nutmeg and sugar. Heat very gently until sugar dissolves, then remove from heat. Let stand 30 minutes to infuse. Strain and return to heat. Bring to just below simmering point and stir in brandy. Serve in glasses with slices of kumquat and freshly ground nutmeg.

Makes 4 to 6 servings.

Banana-Coffee Shakes

1 tablespoon instant coffee granules
2/3 cup boiling water
1 pint vanilla ice cream
1 large banana
1-1/4 cups milk
Few drops vanilla extract
1/3 cup Tia Maria
2 teaspoons finely grated semisweet
   chocolate

In a small bowl, mix coffee and water and cool. In a blender or food processor fitted with the metal blade, process coffee, ice cream, banana, milk, vanilla and Tia Maria until smooth. Pour into tall glasses and sprinkle with grated chocolate.

Makes 4 to 6 servings.

Tangy Punch

1 cup pineapple juice
1 cup grapefruit juice
Juice of 1 lemon
2 cups carbonated water
2 to 4 teaspoons mint syrup
Ice cubes
Pineapple chunks
Sprigs of mint and pineapple wedges to
 decorate

Mix pineapple, grapefruit and lemon juices, carbonated water and mint syrup in a large pitcher. Fill glasses with large ice cubes and pineapple chunks. Pour in punch and decorate each with a sprig of mint and a wedge of fresh pineapple.

Makes 4 to 6 servings.

MENU I
Sausage & Apple Braid, page 10
Breakfast Kabobs, page 11
Kedgeree, page 22
Apple-Cinnamon Waffles, page 27
Spiced Orange Tea, page 107

MENU II
Prosciutto & Figs, page 29
Brioche, page 30
Peach Melba Hearts, page 33
Rose Petal Infusion, page 109

MENU III
Maple Crunch Cereal, page 45
Herb Baked Eggs, page 48
Chewy Fruit Bars, page 47
Peach Cooler, page 108

MENU IV
Sausage & Bean Rolls, page 54
Soufflé-Filled Tomatoes, page 55
Sunday Treats, page 57
Hash Browns with Tomato Relish, page 59
Banana & Strawberry Drop Scones, page 65
Tangy Punch, page 113

MENU V
Pear & Loganberry Soup, page 74
Shrimp & Mushroom Barquettes, page 71
Sausage Covered Eggs, page 83
Pinwheels, page 78
Lemon Geranium Syllabub, page 85
Tropical Cocktail, page 104

MENU VI
Mushroom Bundles, page 88
Chicken & Asparagus Terrine, page 89
Cucumber-Shrimp Mousse, page 93
Gazpacho, page 96
Danish Windmill Pastries, page 99
Champagne & Mint Gratina, page 103
Raspberry Cooler, page 110

INDEX